Beach Blessings:

A photographic journey of awakening to the beauty and blessings of the ocean

By Jackie Tury

Beach Blessings: A photographic journey of awakening to the beauty and blessings of the ocean.

All words and images copyright ©2015 by Jackie Tury. All rights reserved.

No part of this book may be used or reproduced in any manner without written permission.

Book design by Paul Tury

For information contact Jackie Tury at *jackietury@gmail.com*.

ISBN-13: 978-1514270134

ISBN-10: 1514270137

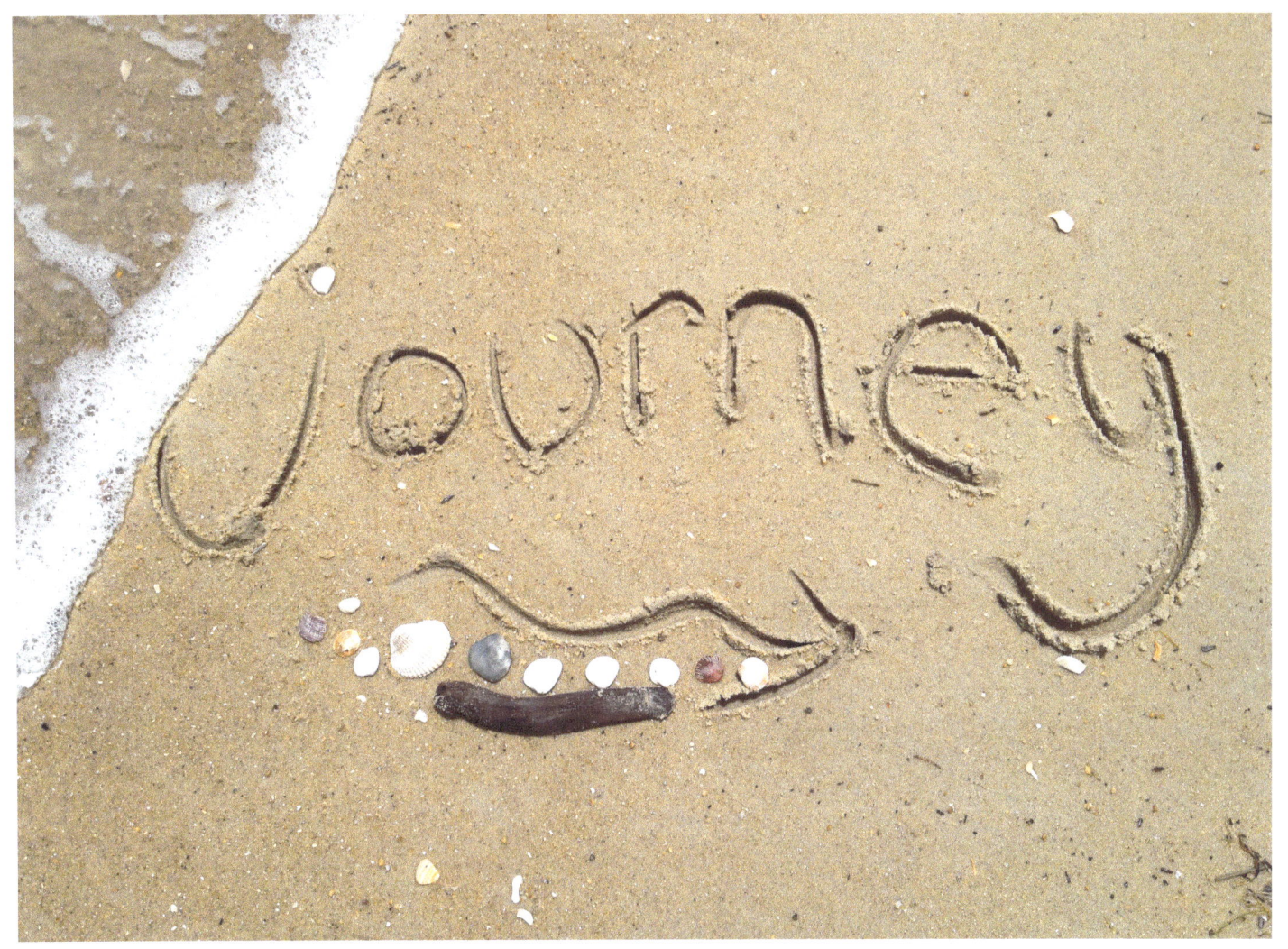

Beach Blessings:

A photographic journey of awakening to the beauty and blessings of the ocean

By Jackie Tury

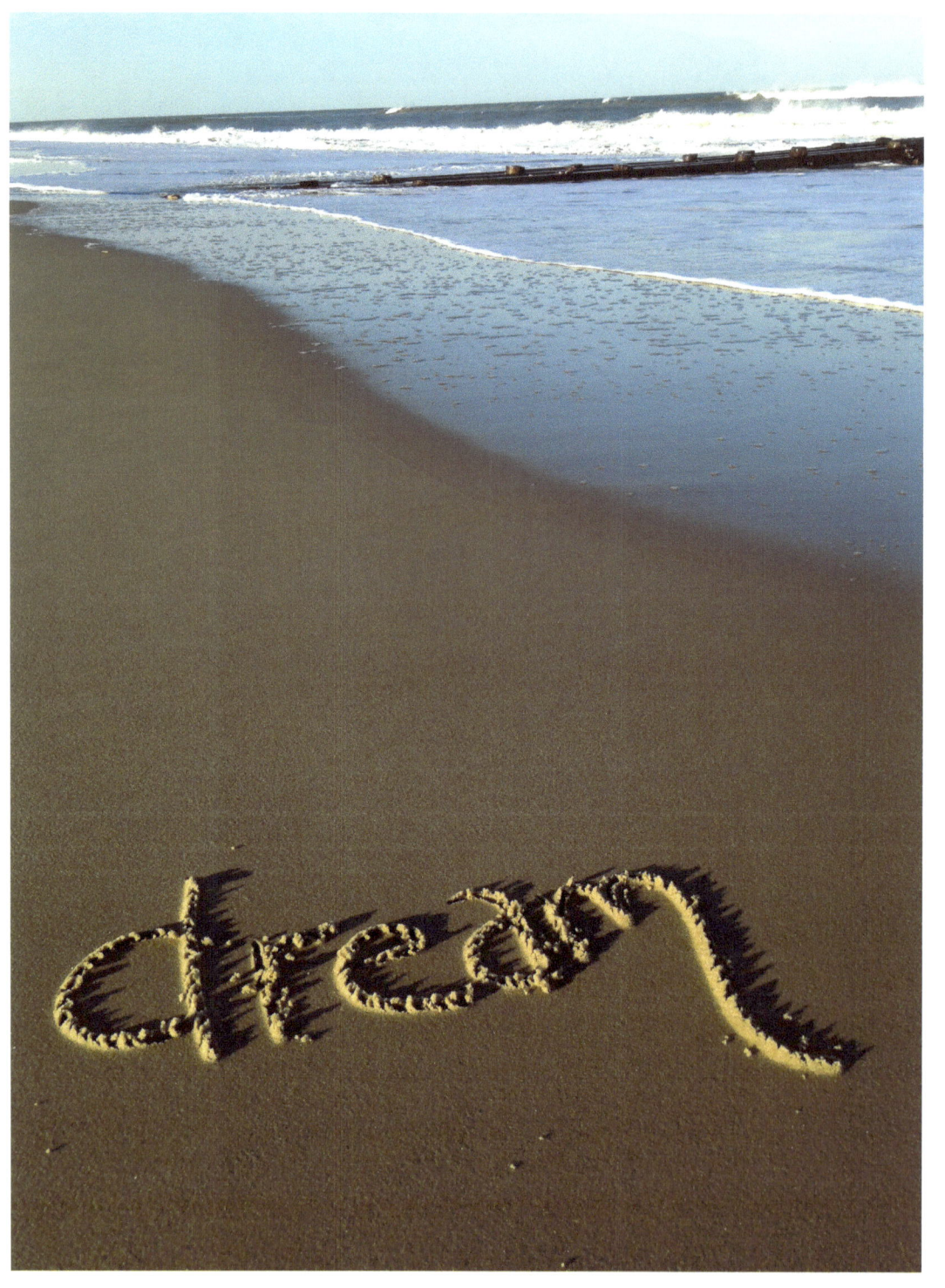

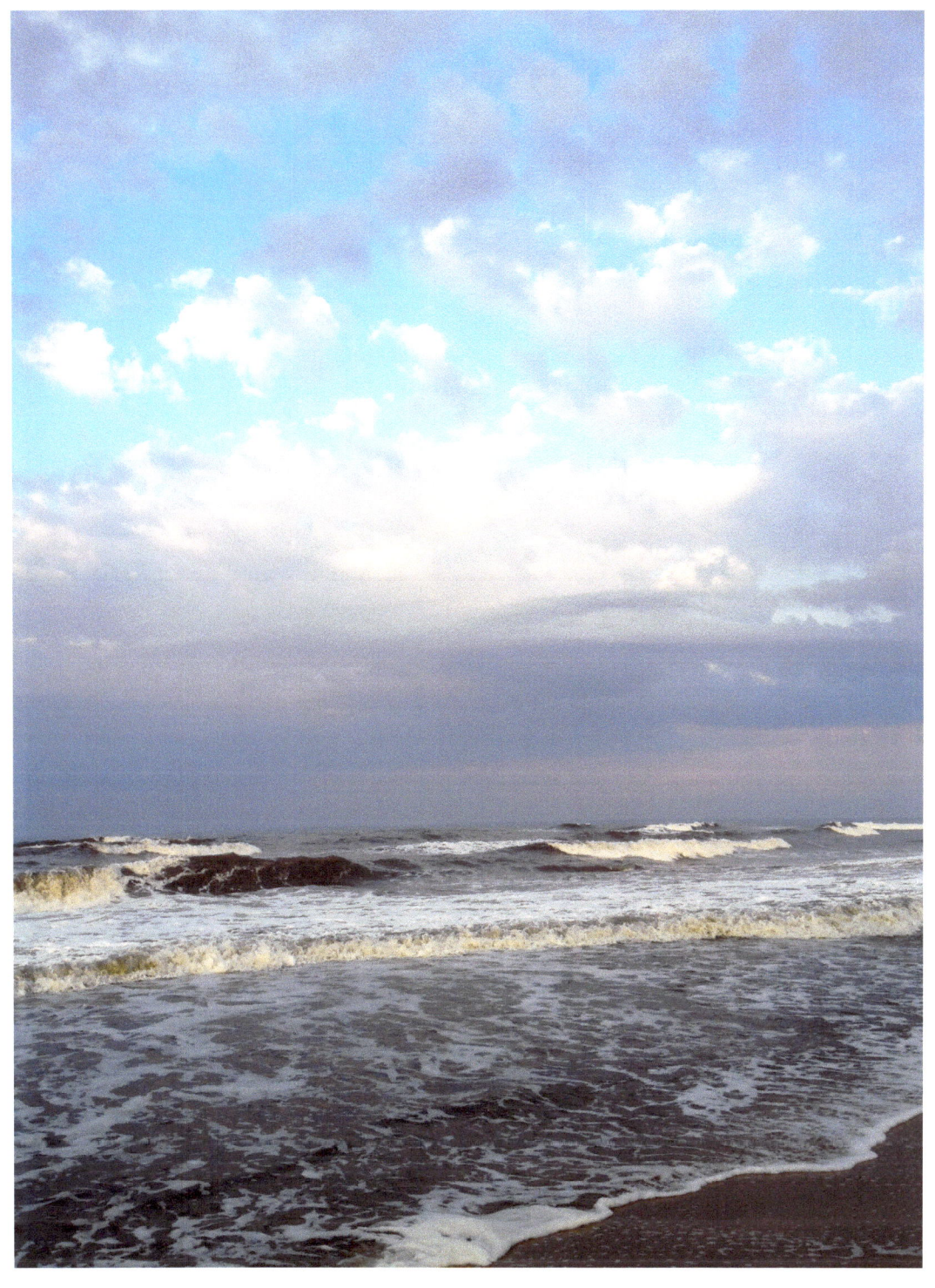

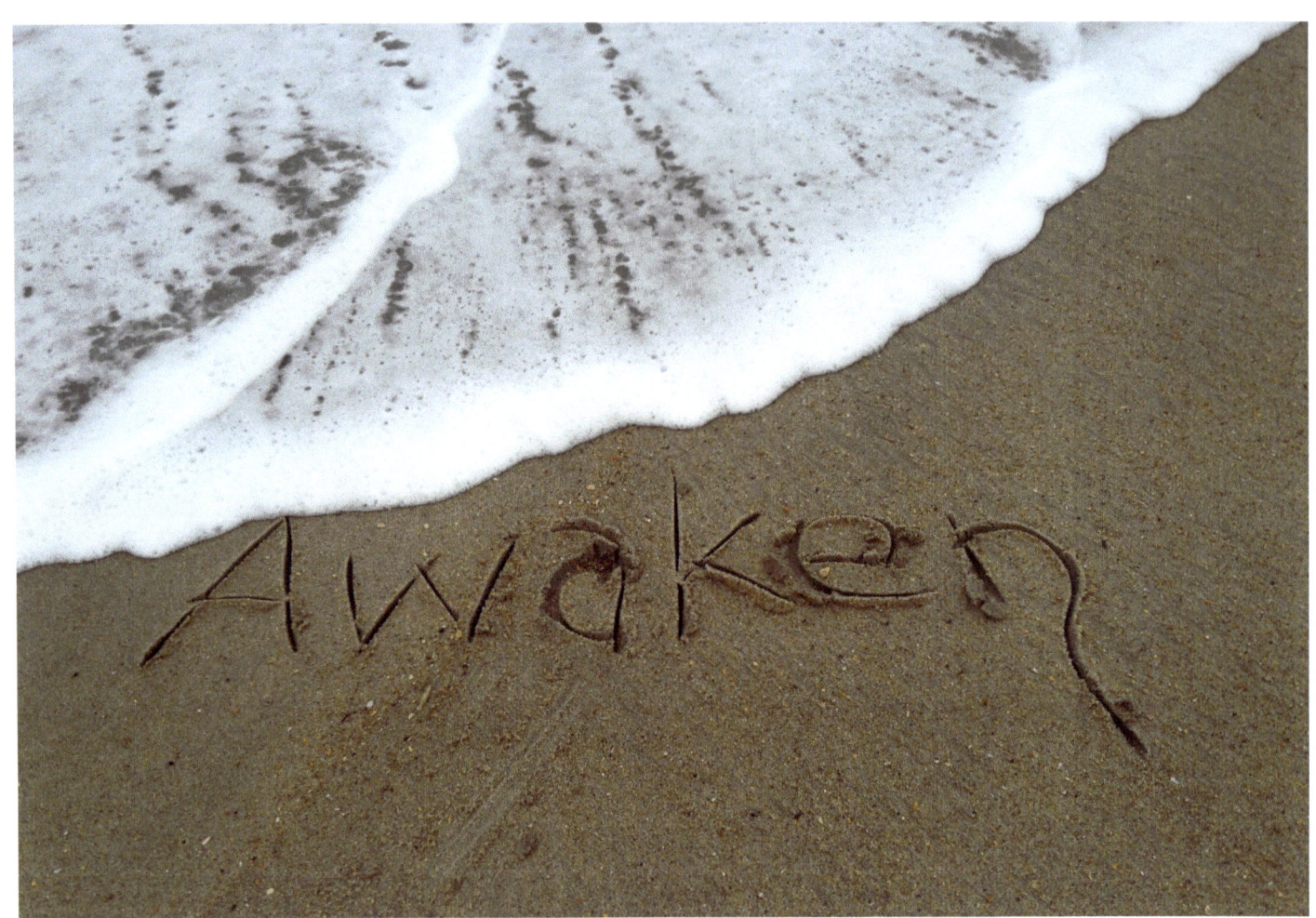

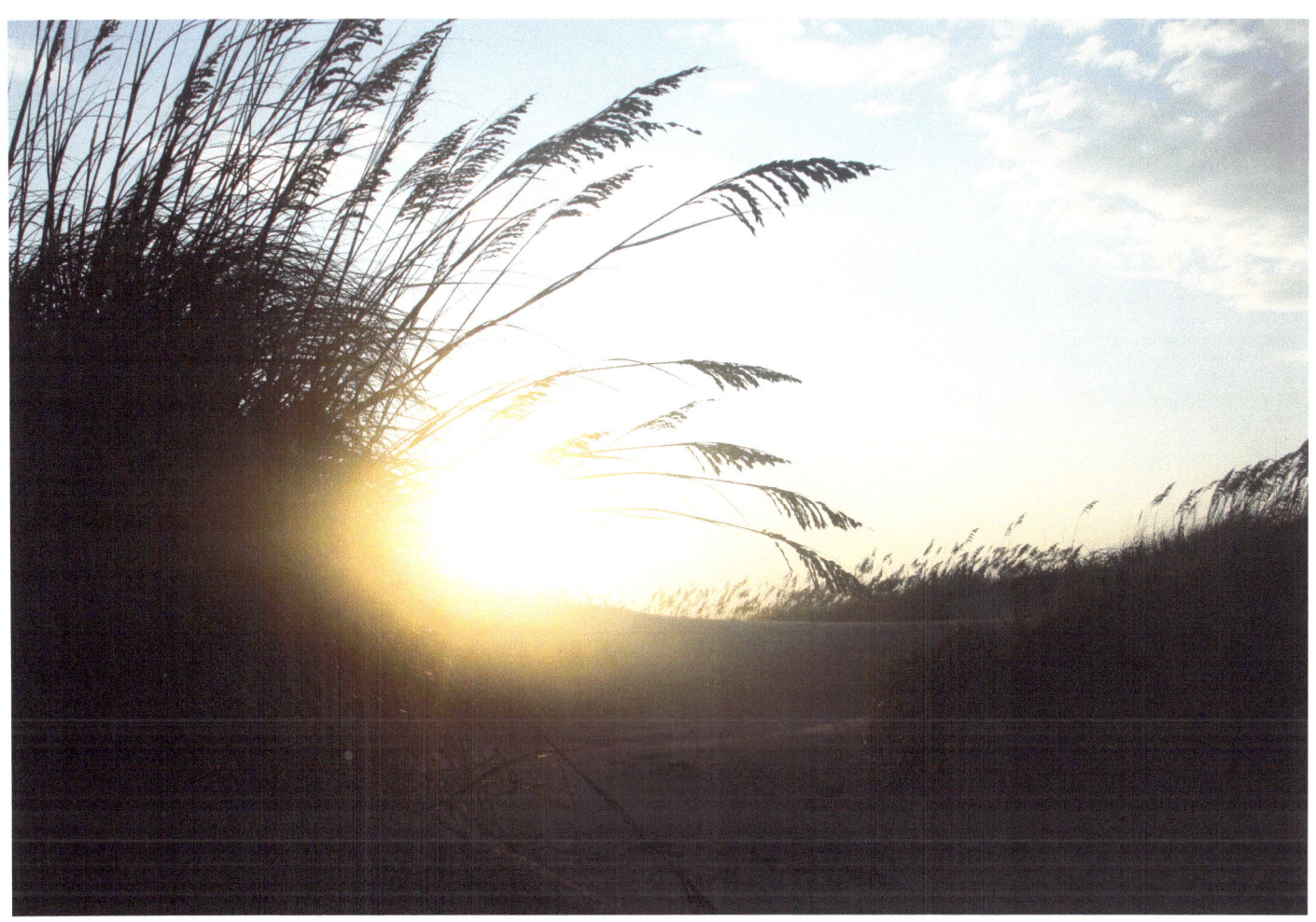

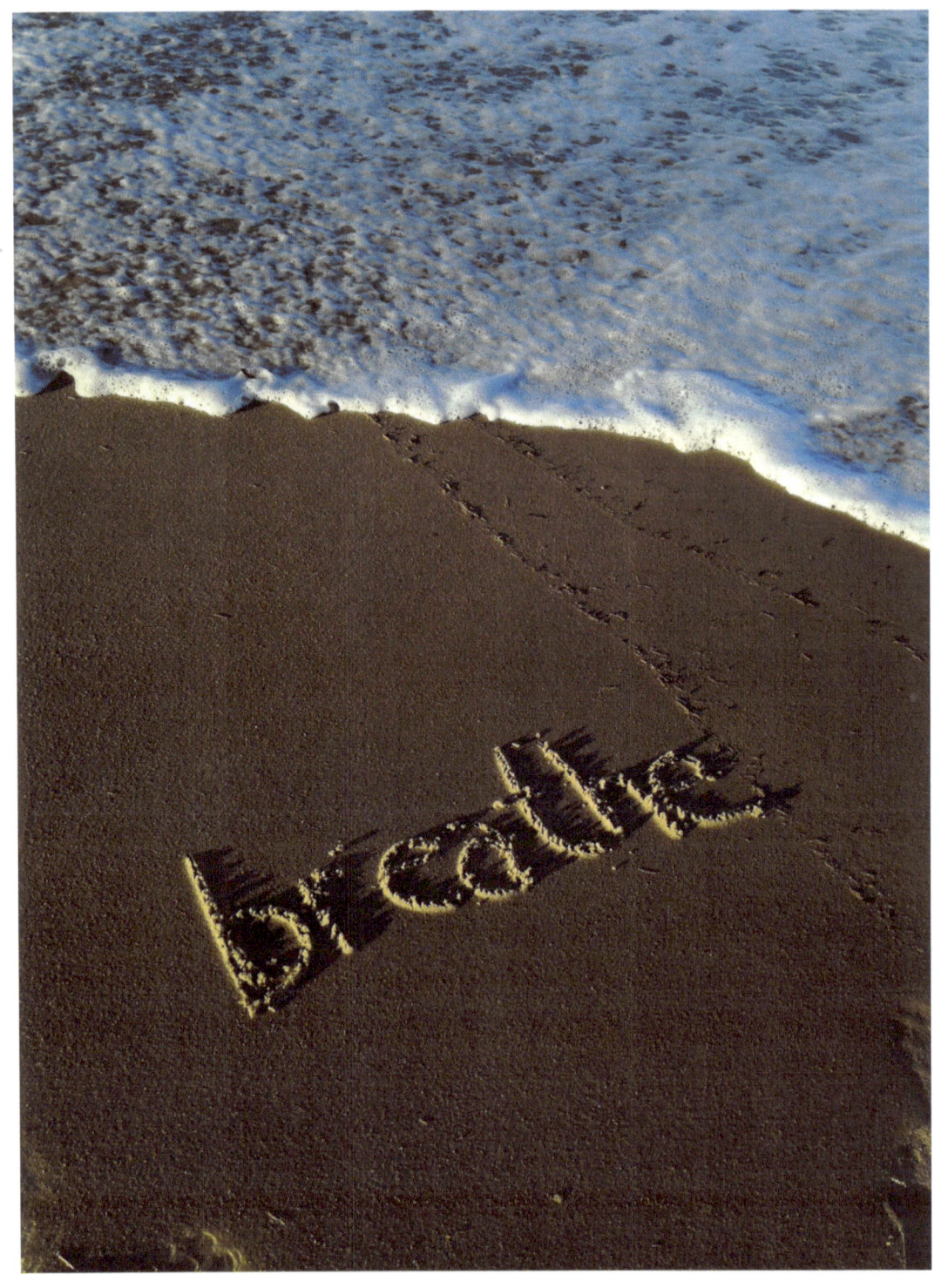

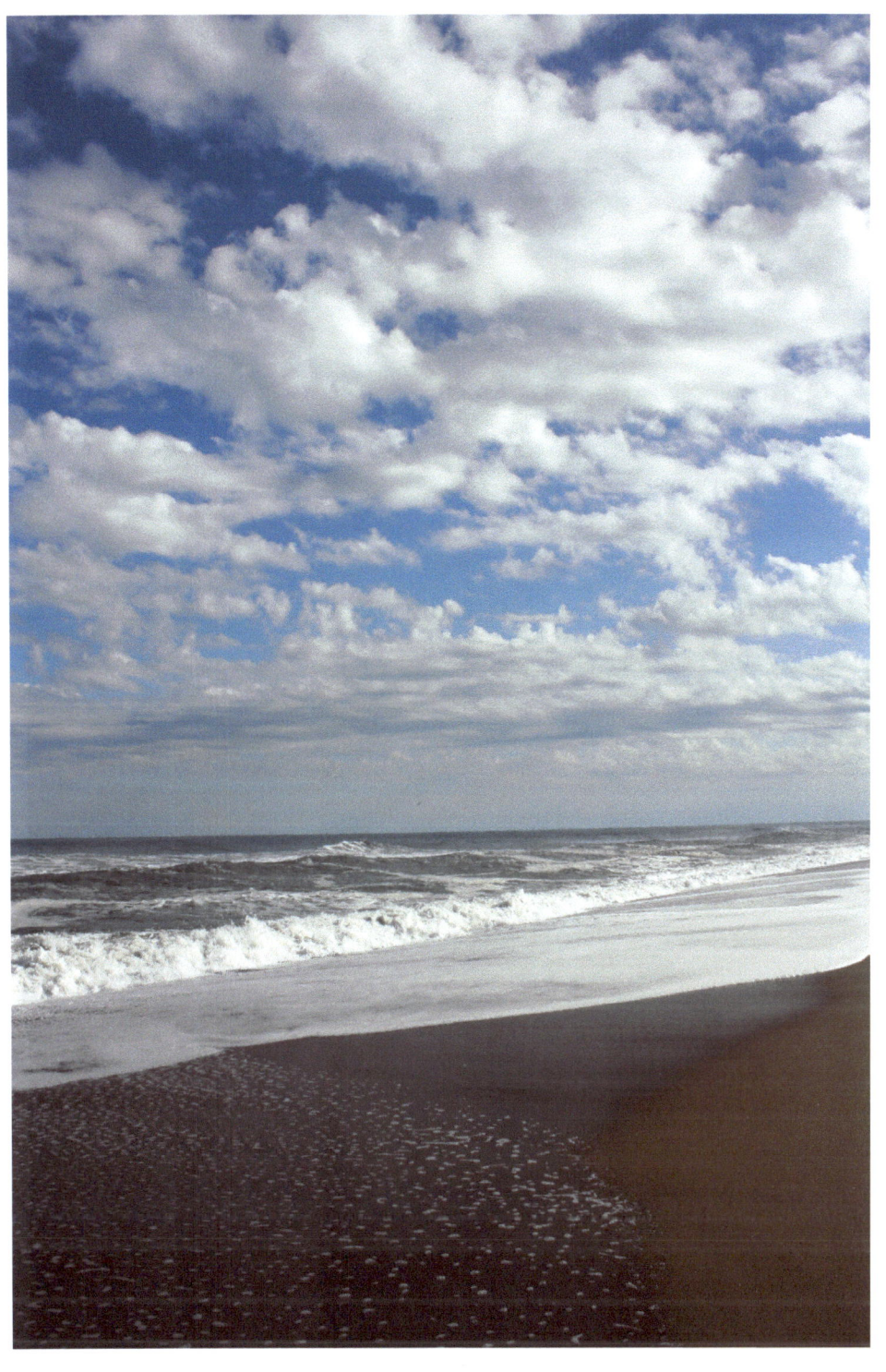

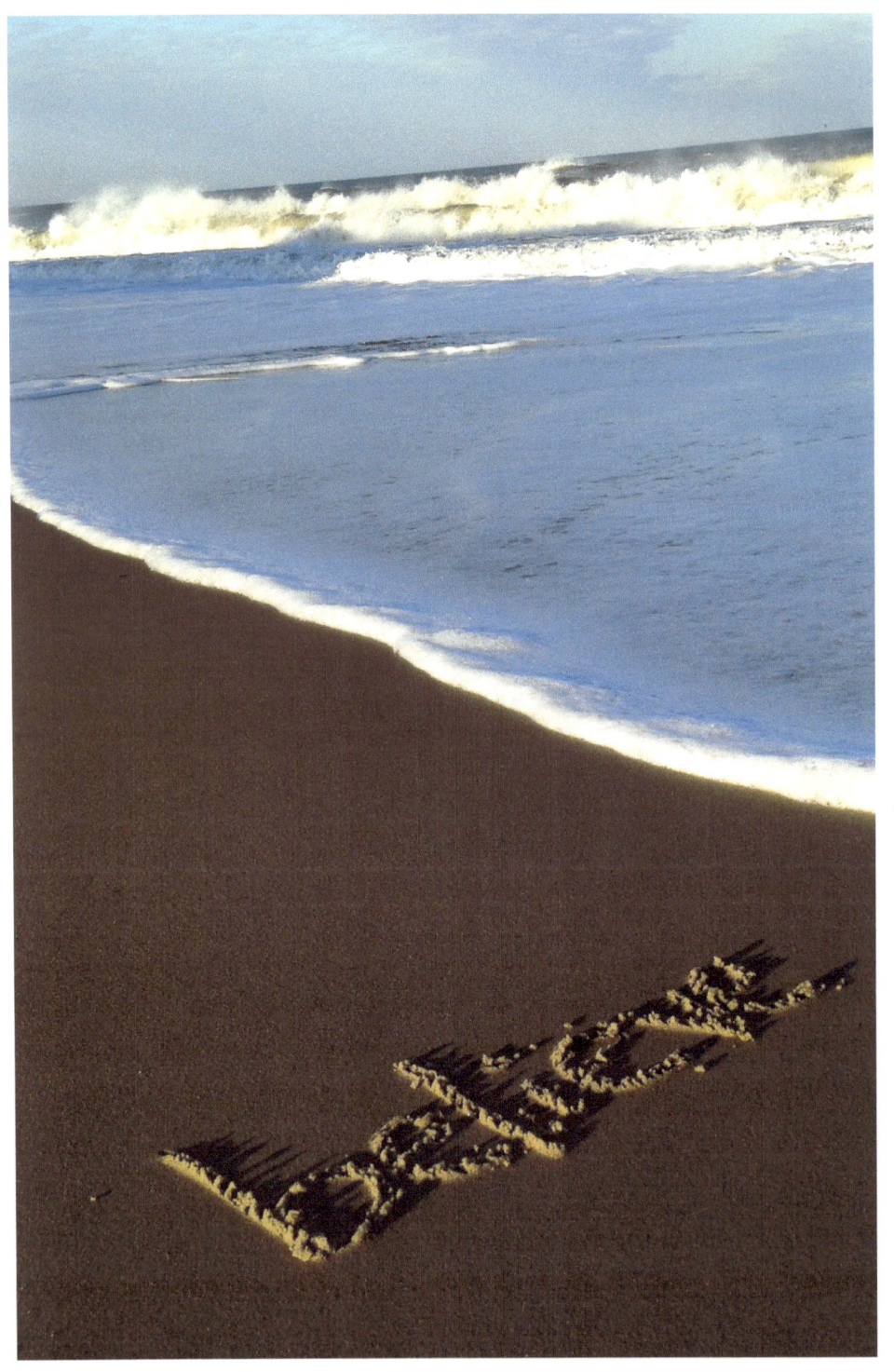

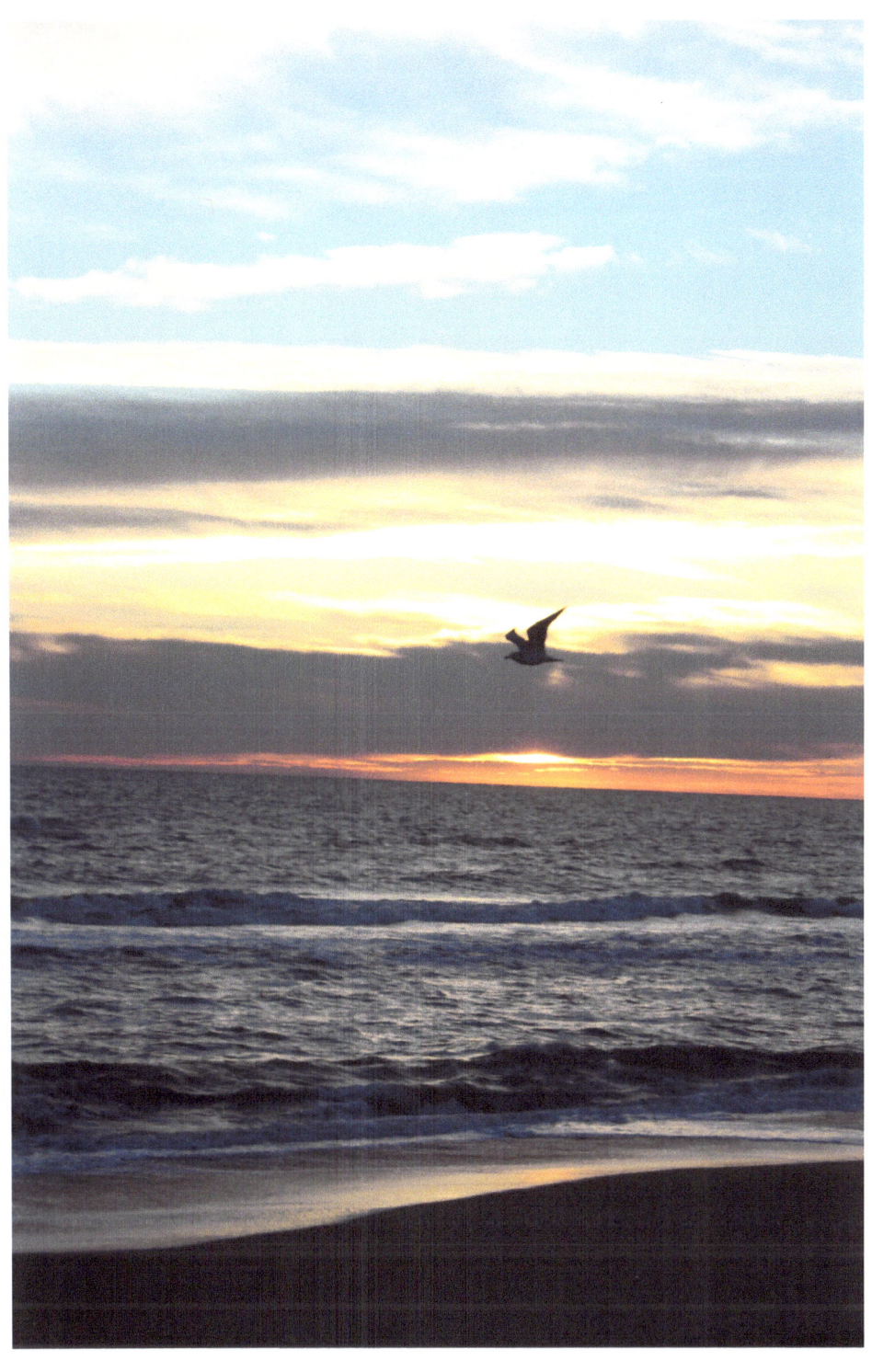

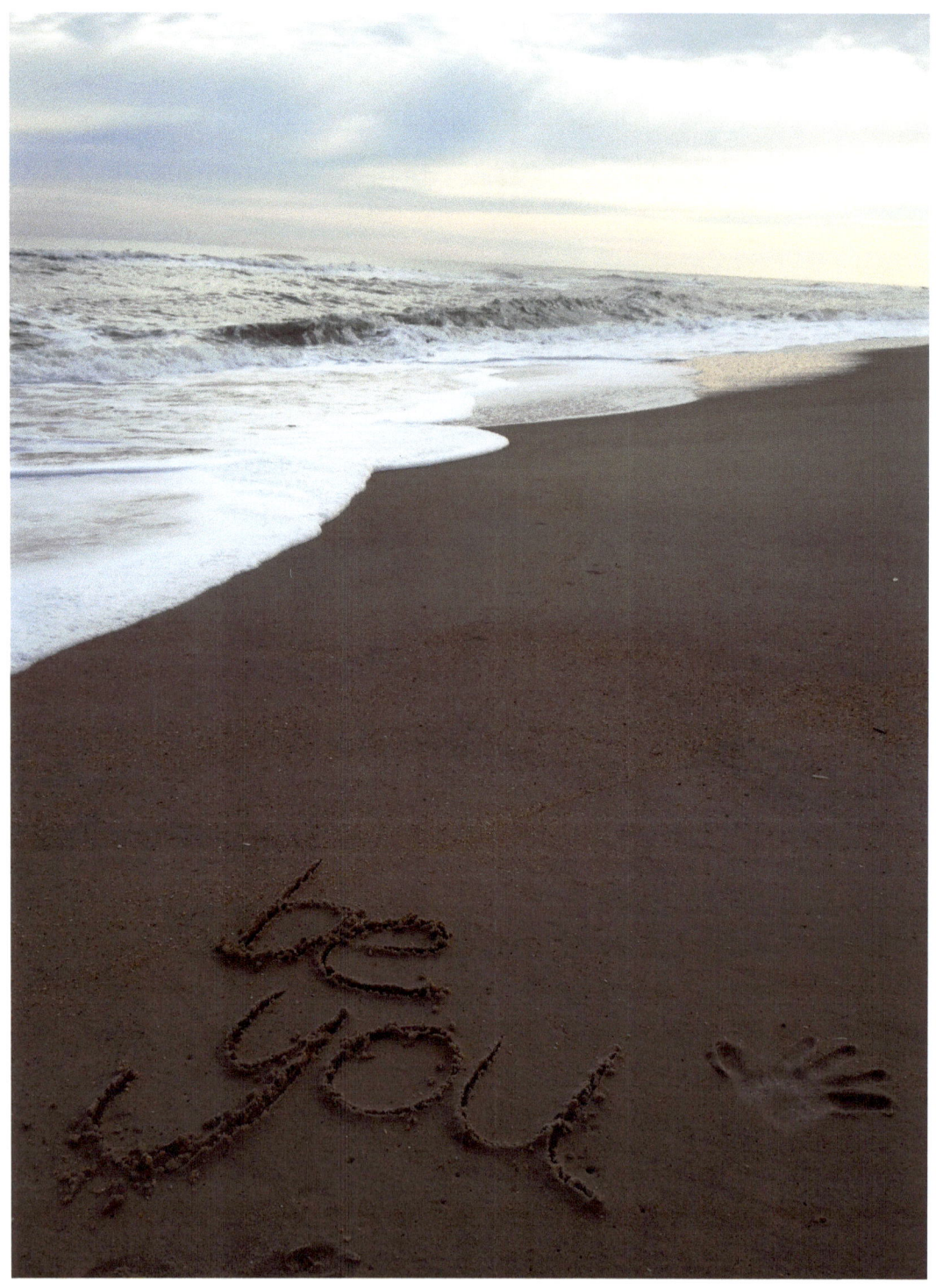

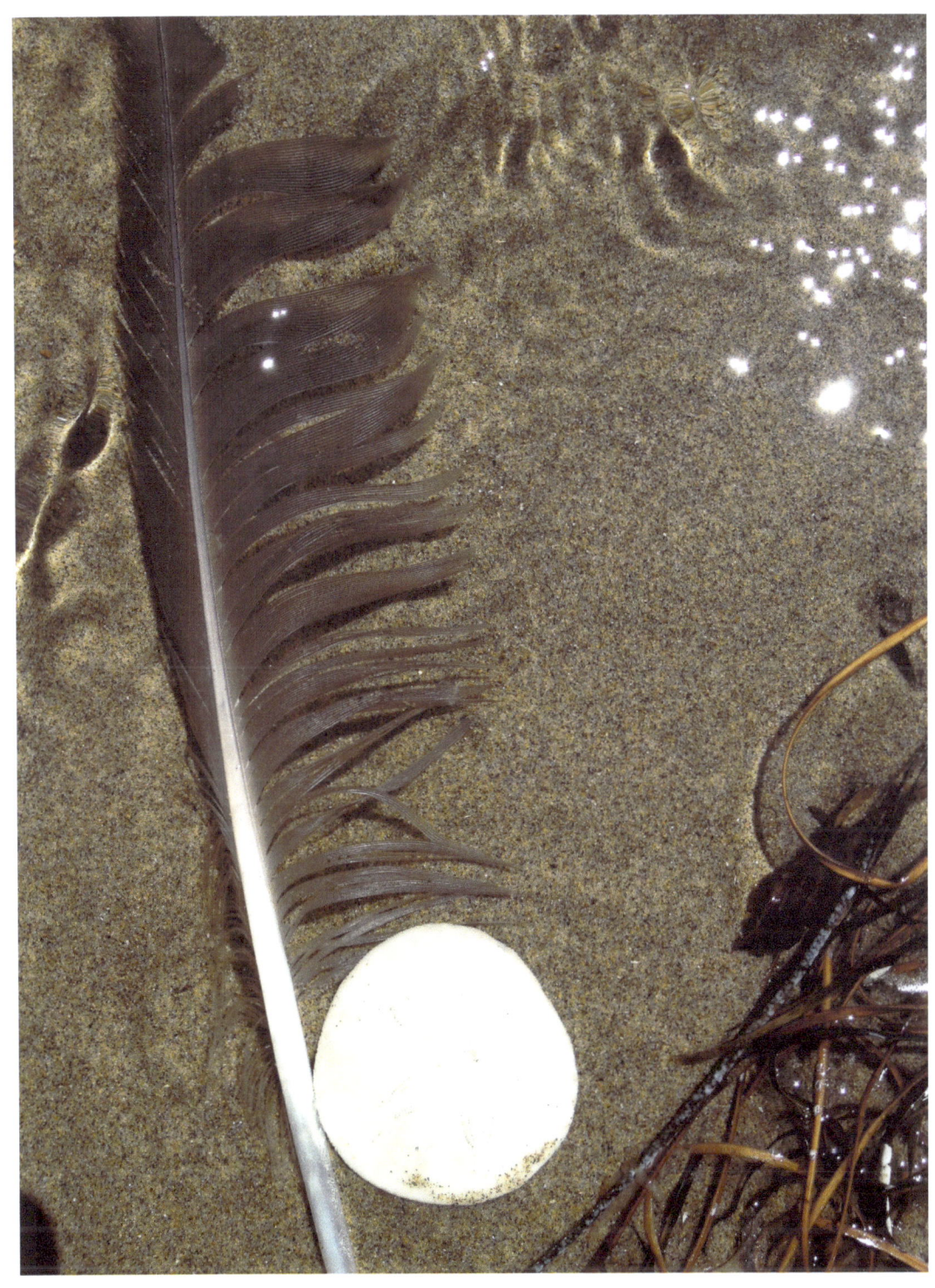

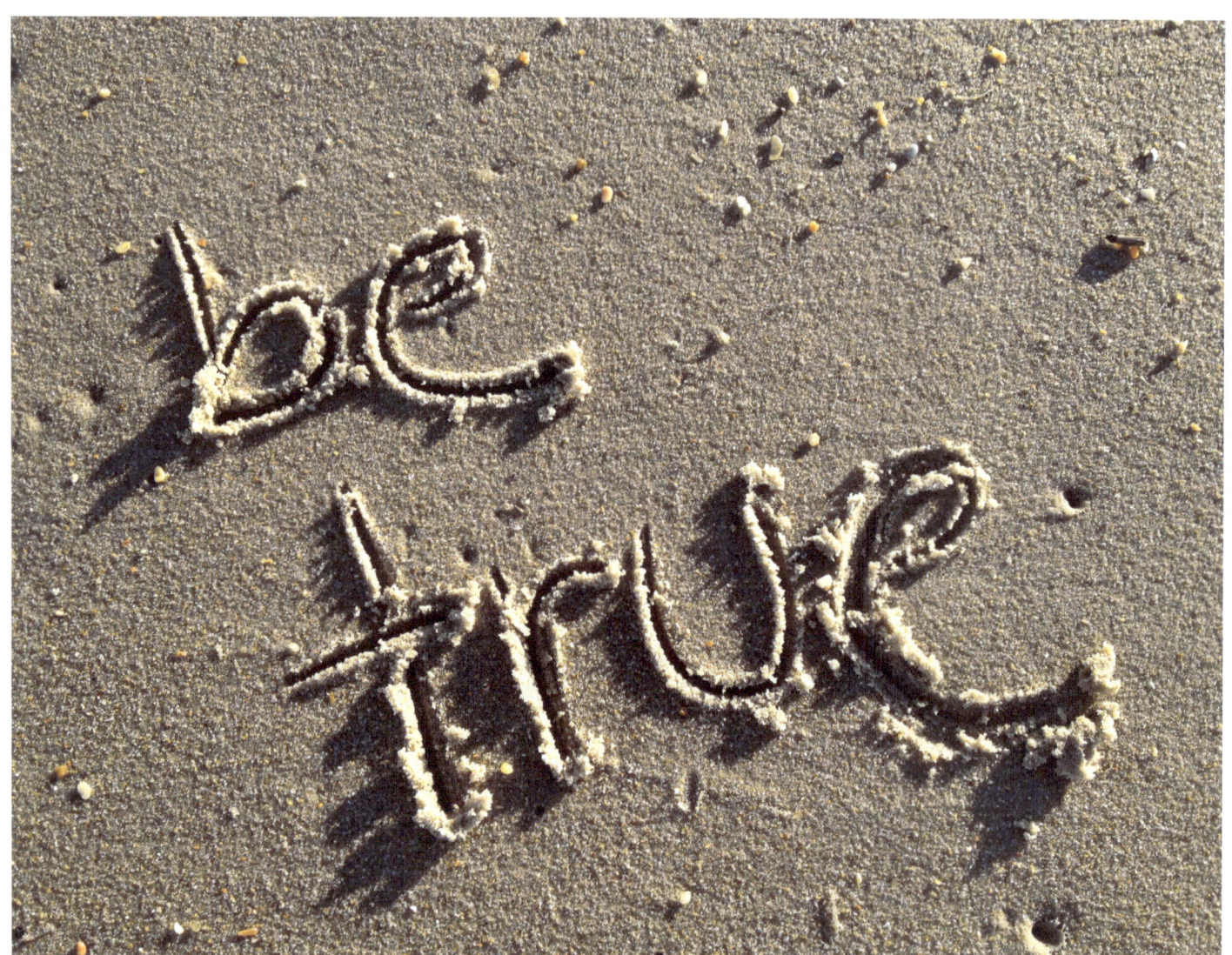

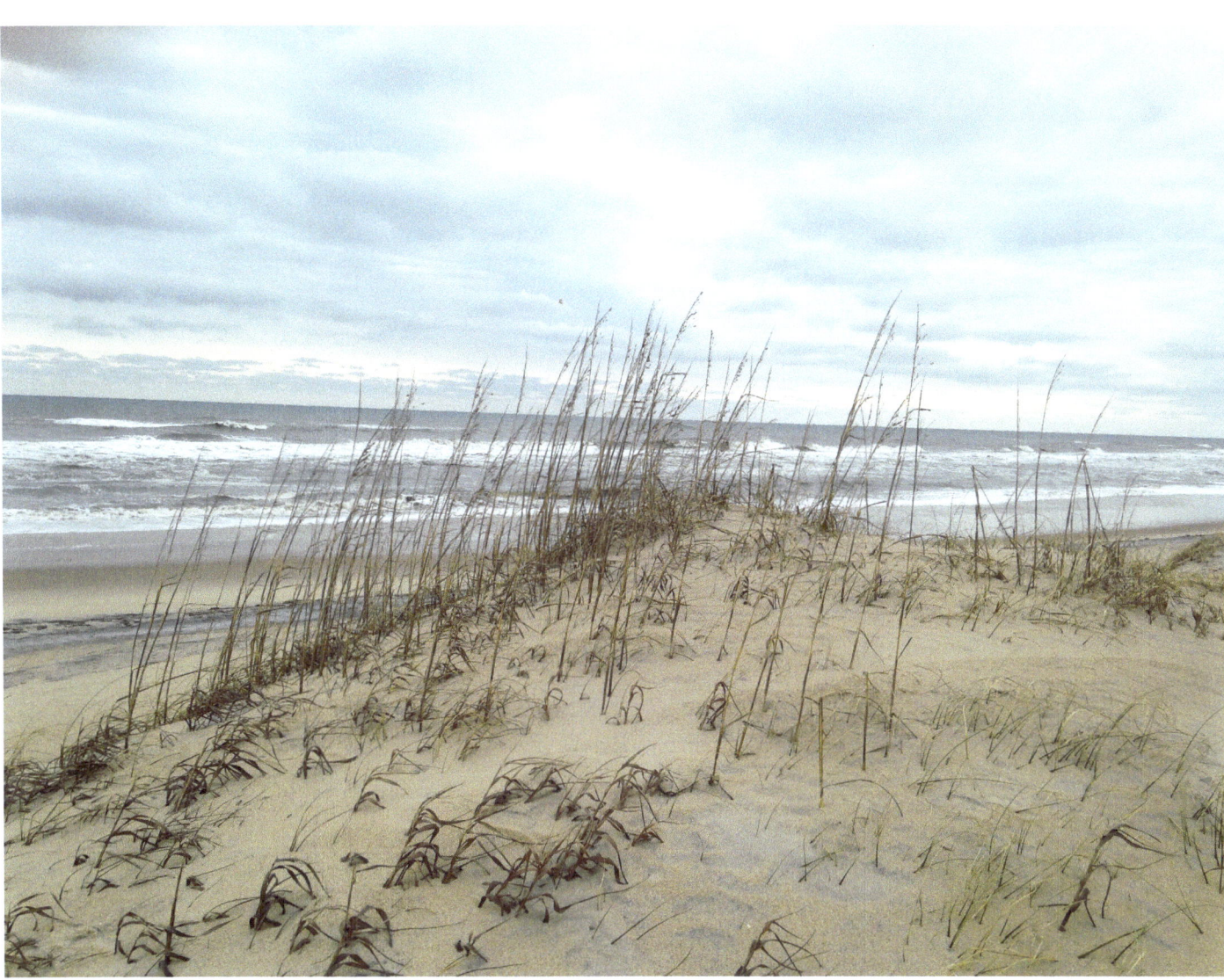

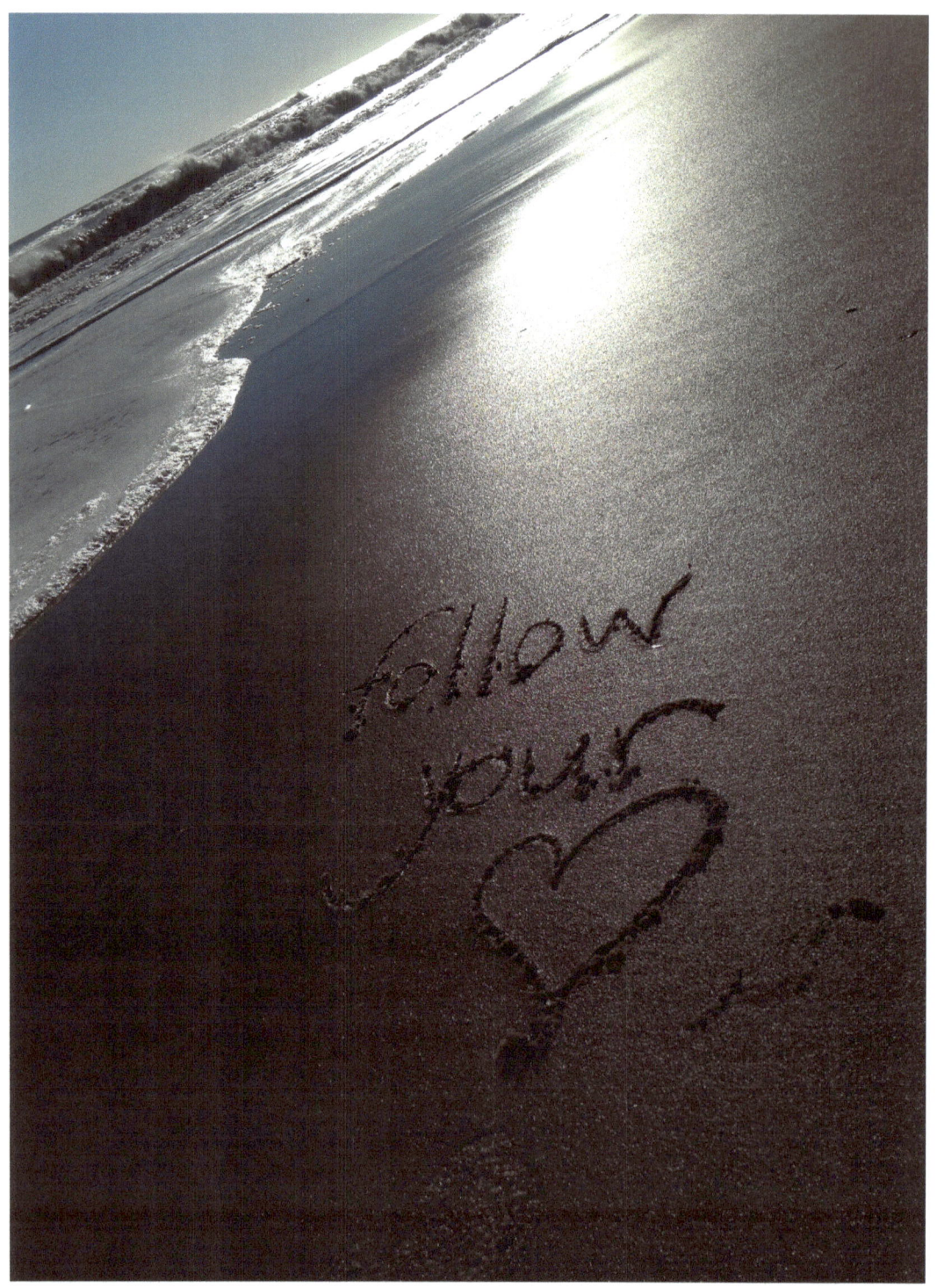

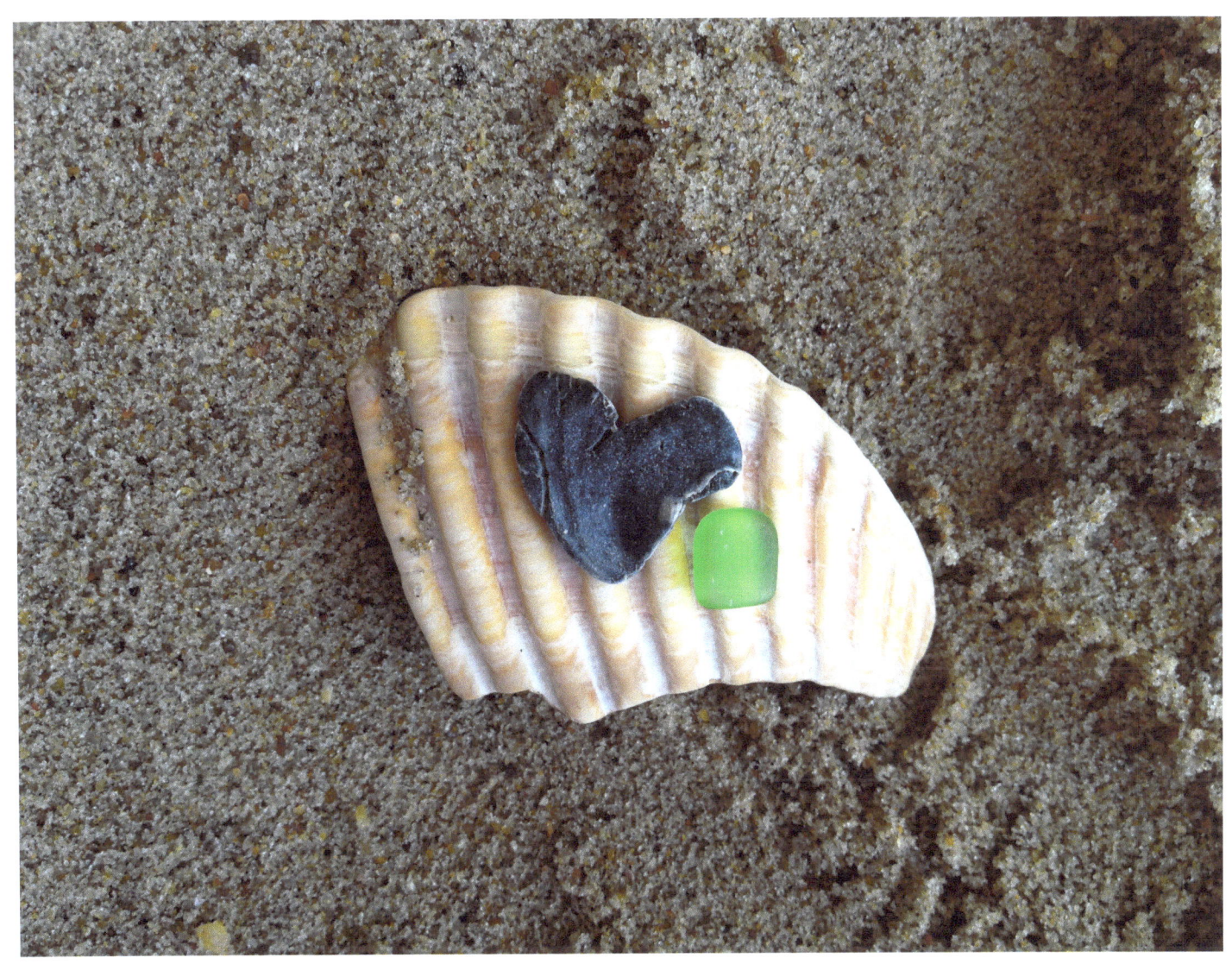

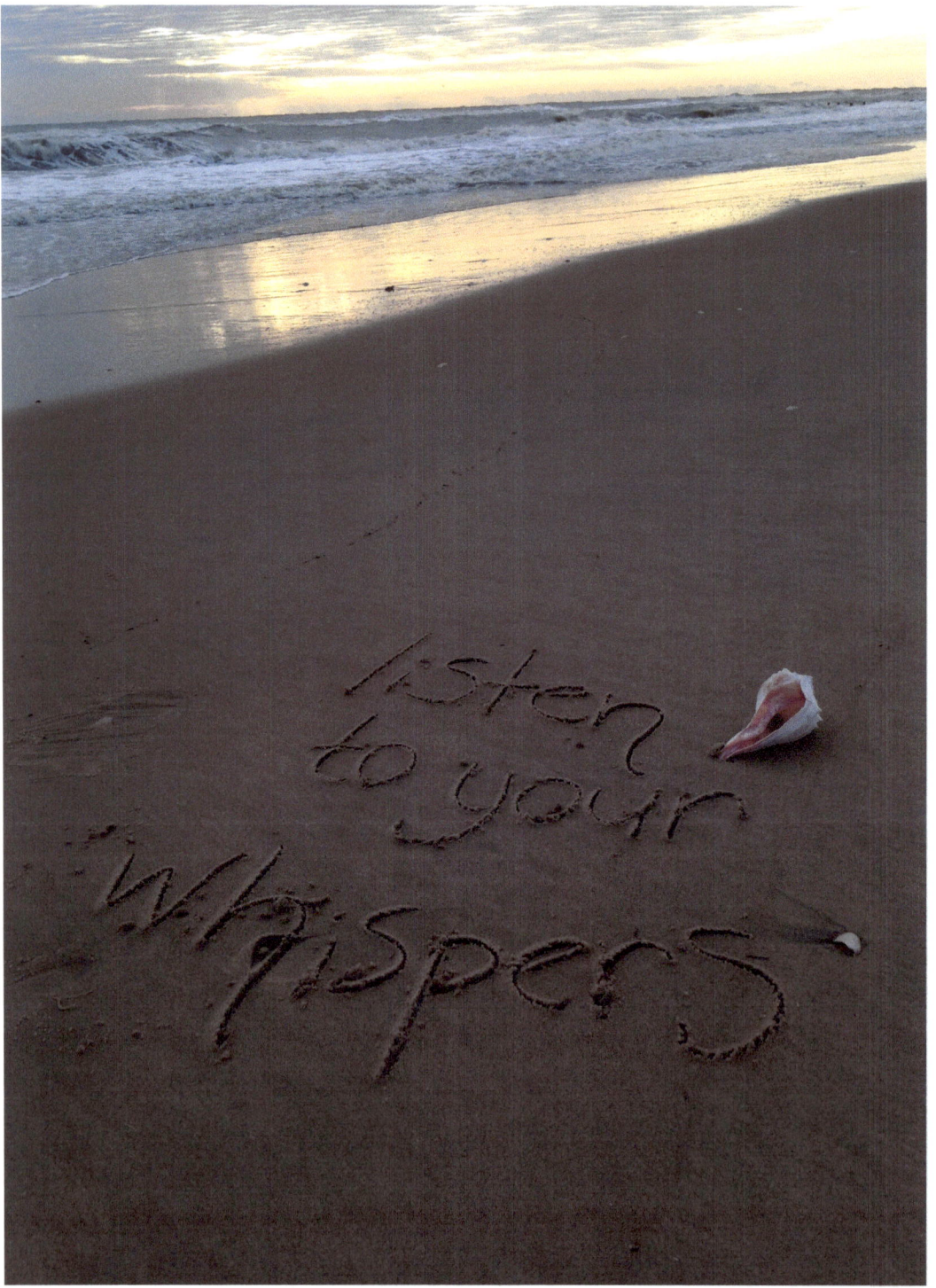

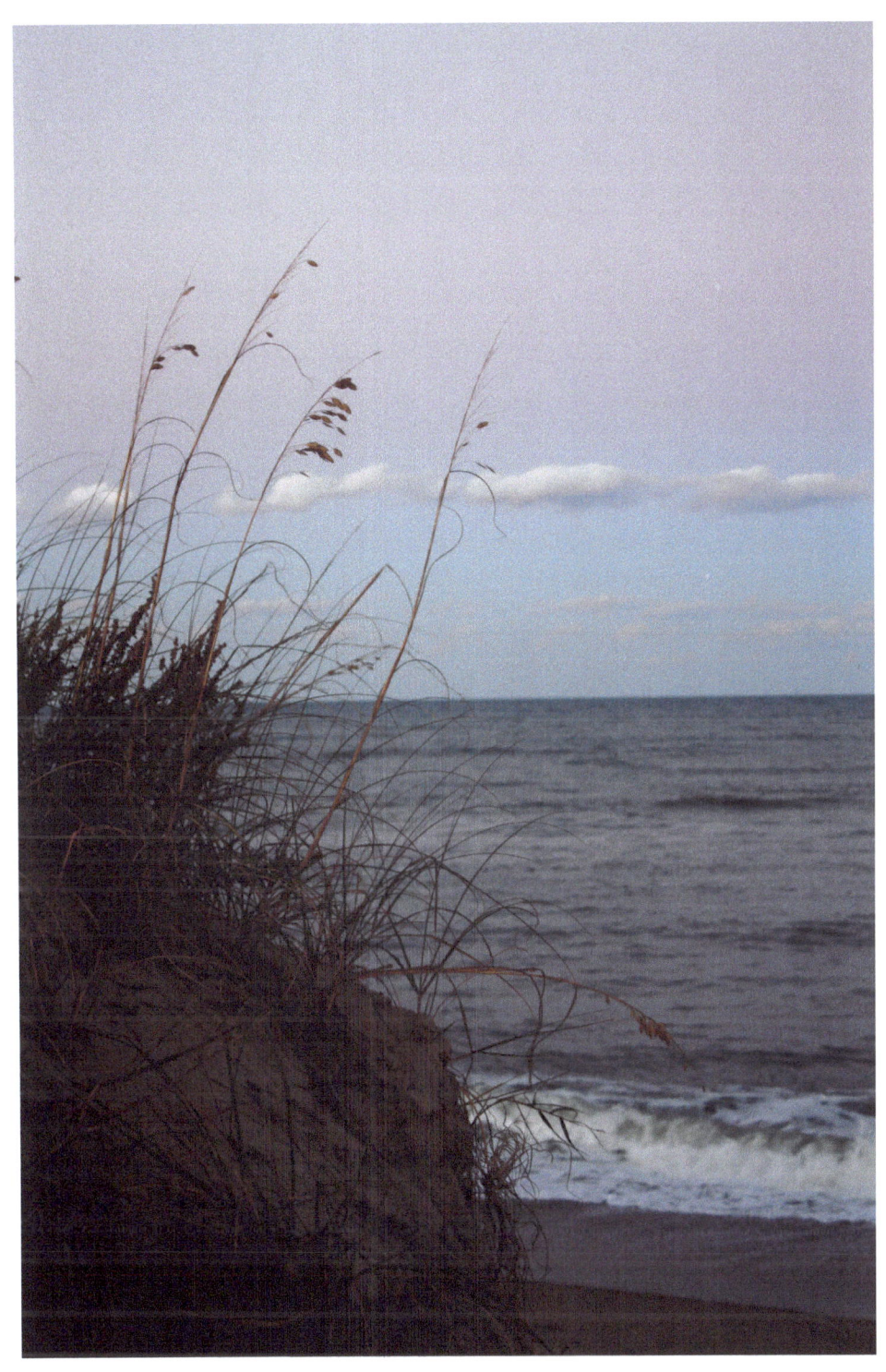

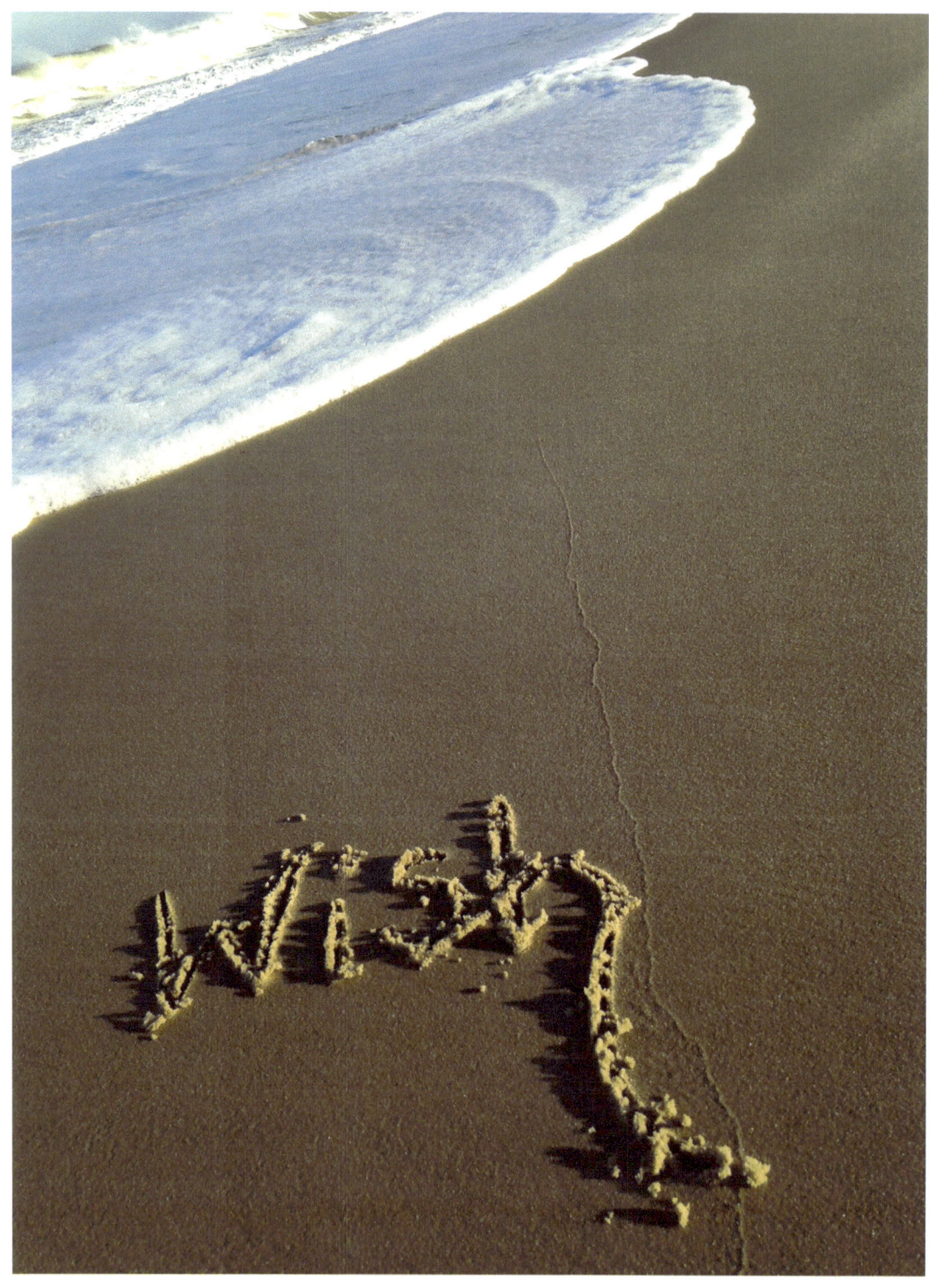

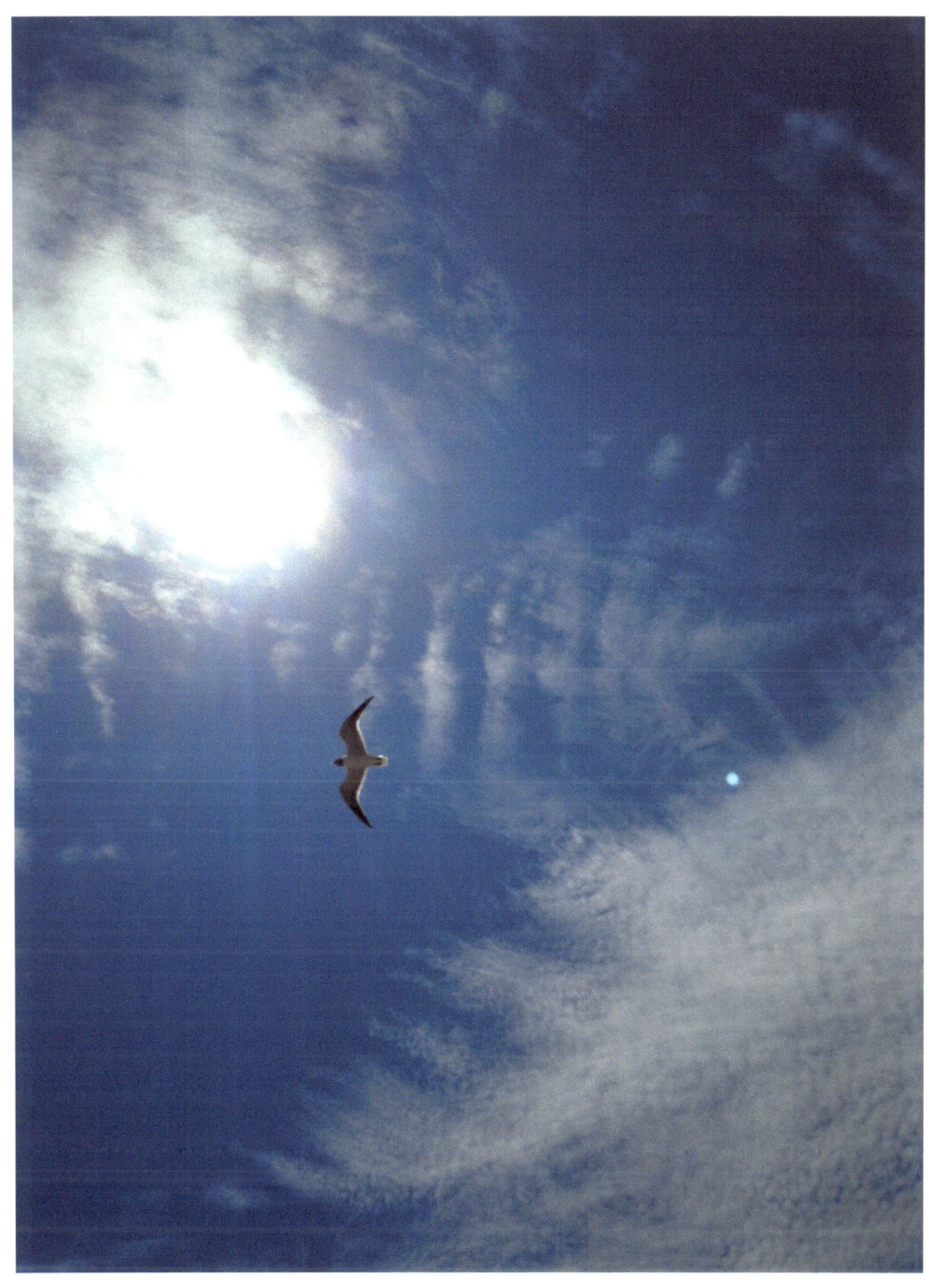

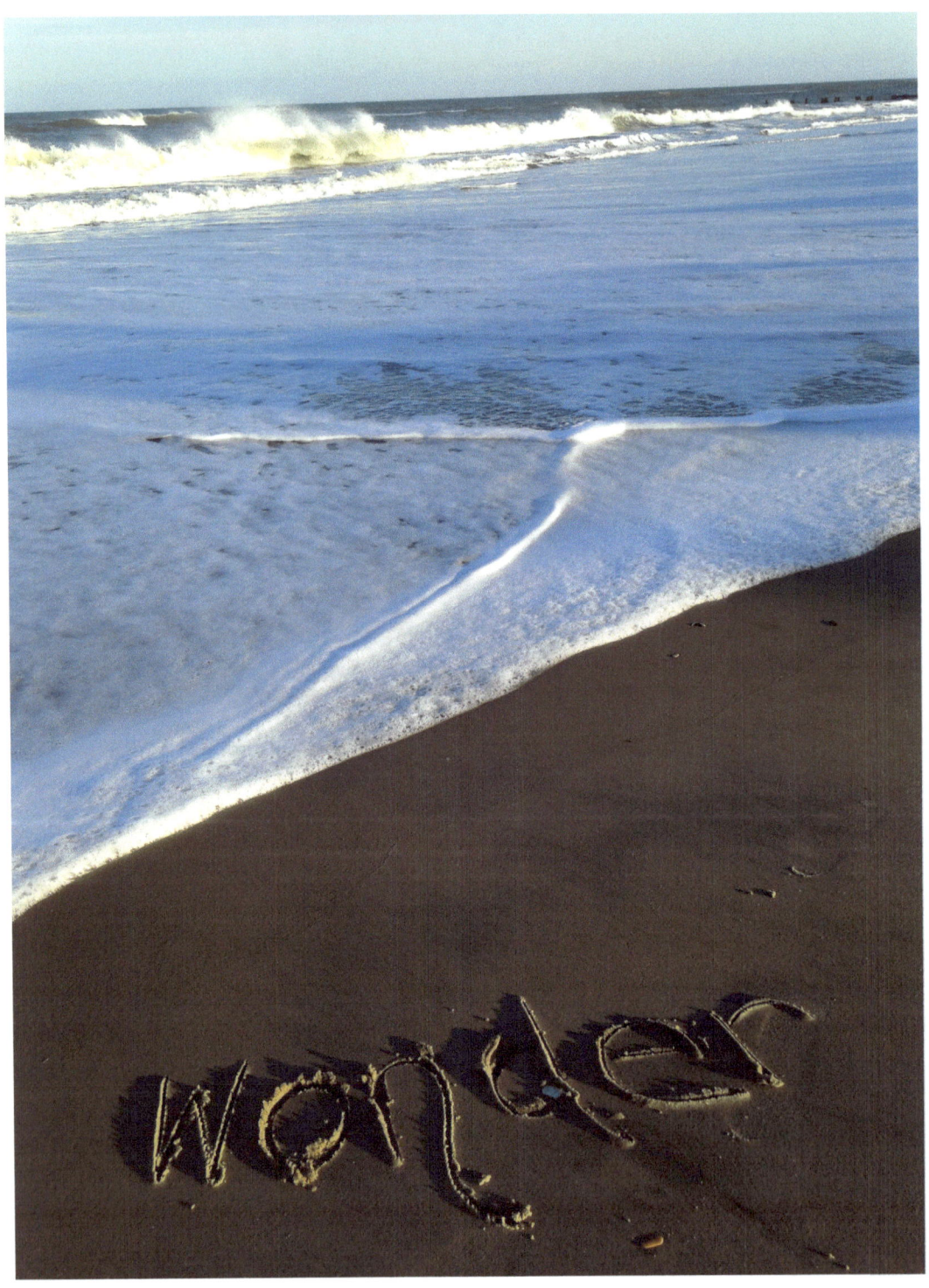

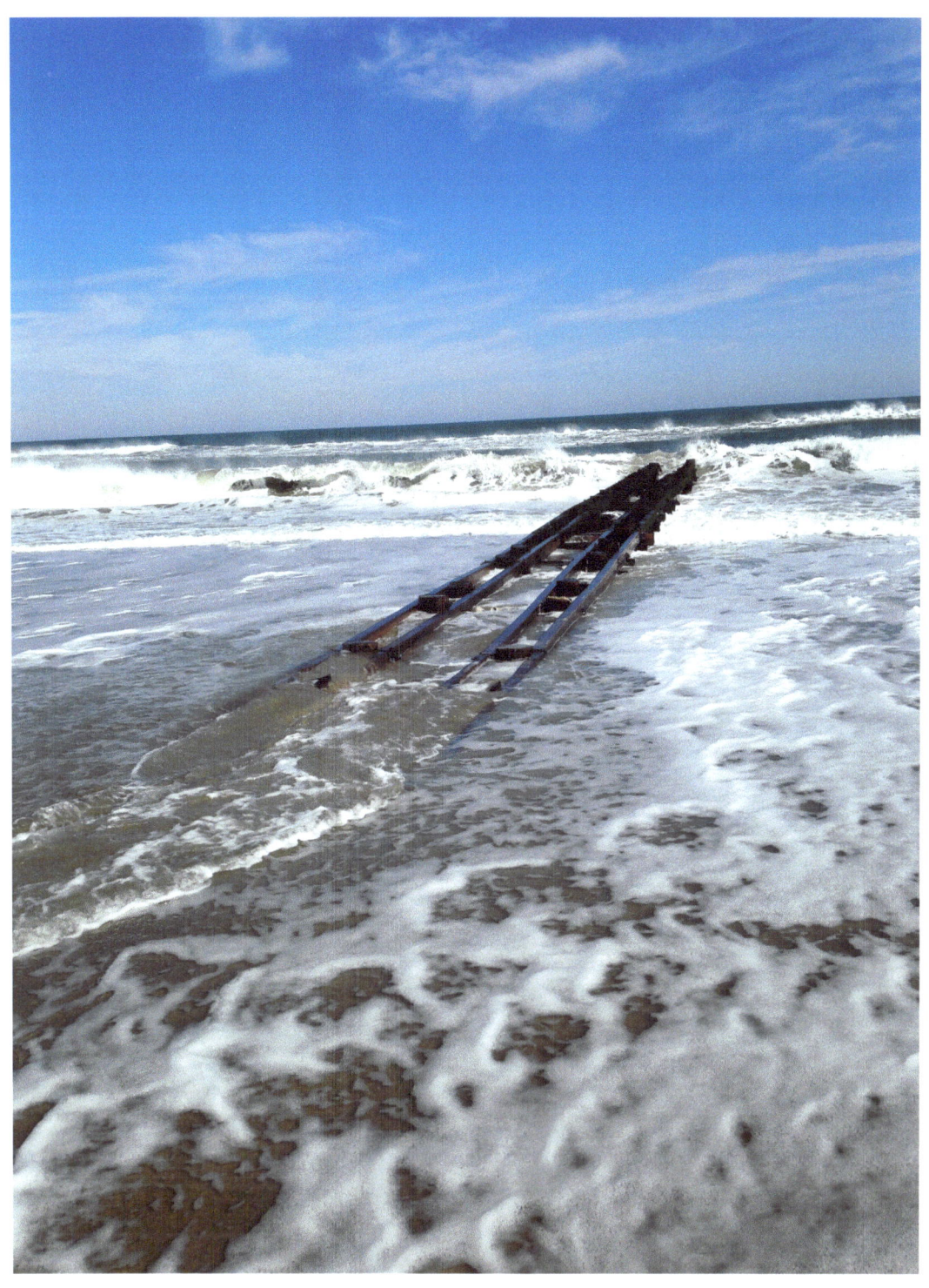

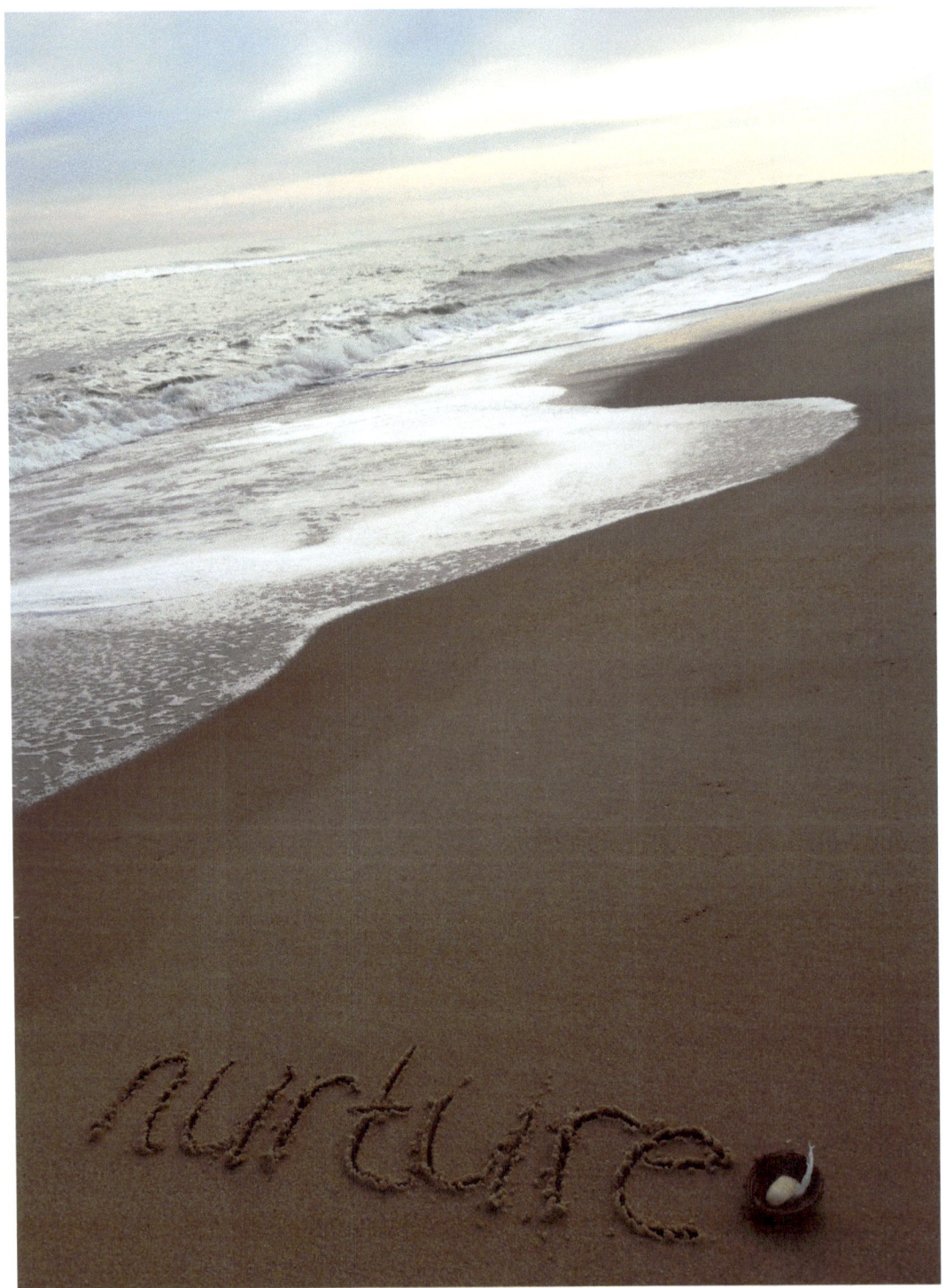

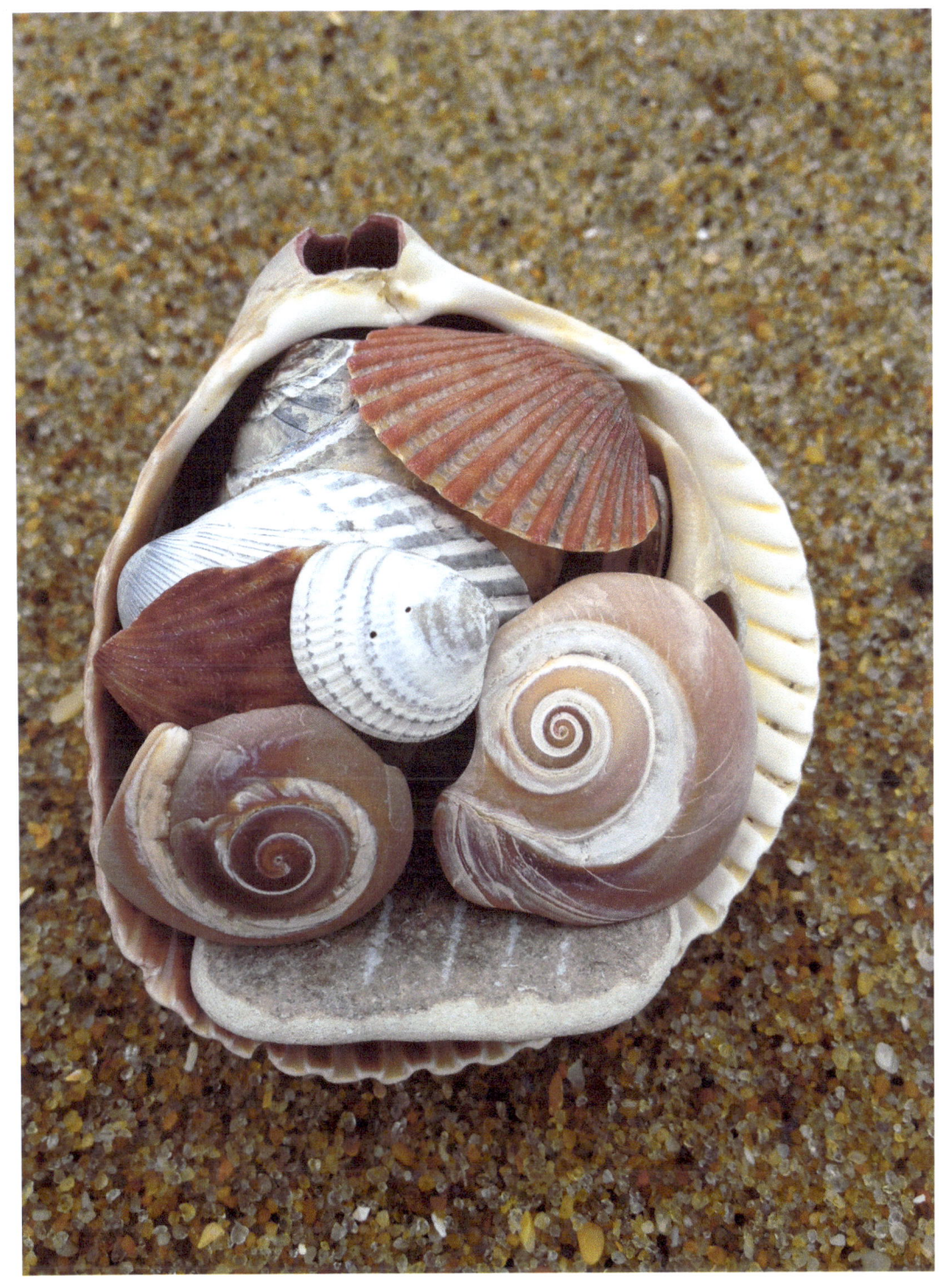

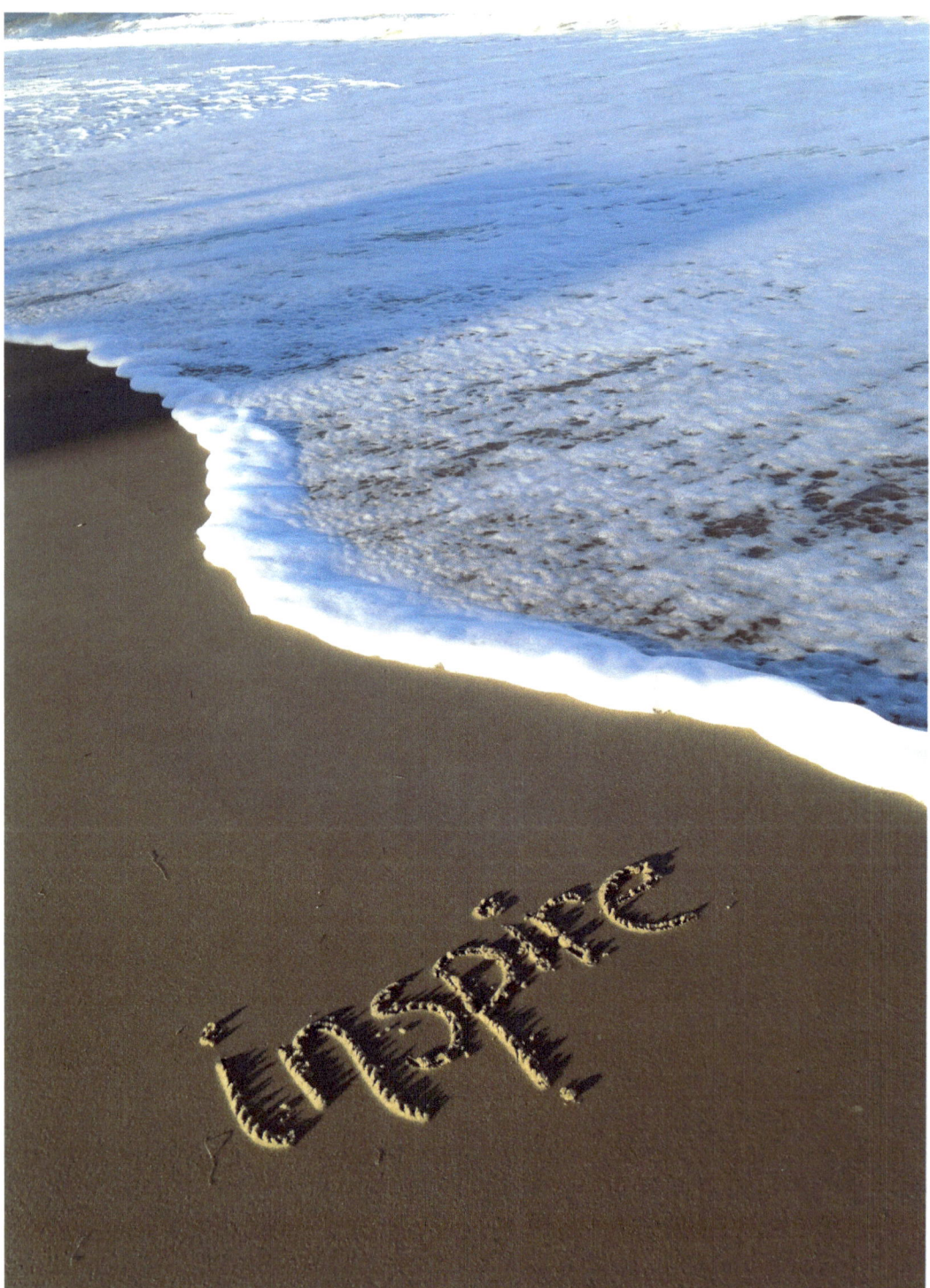

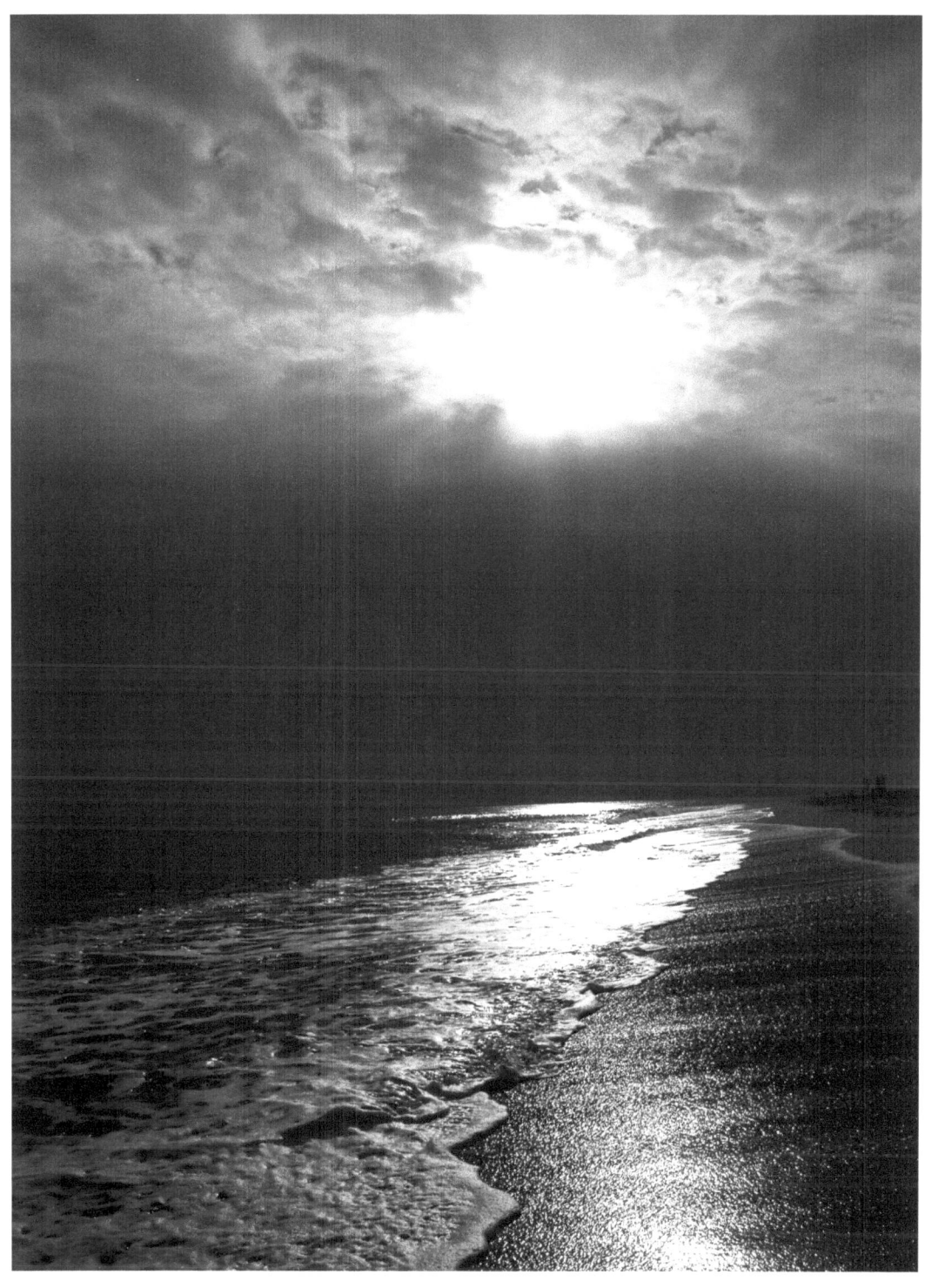

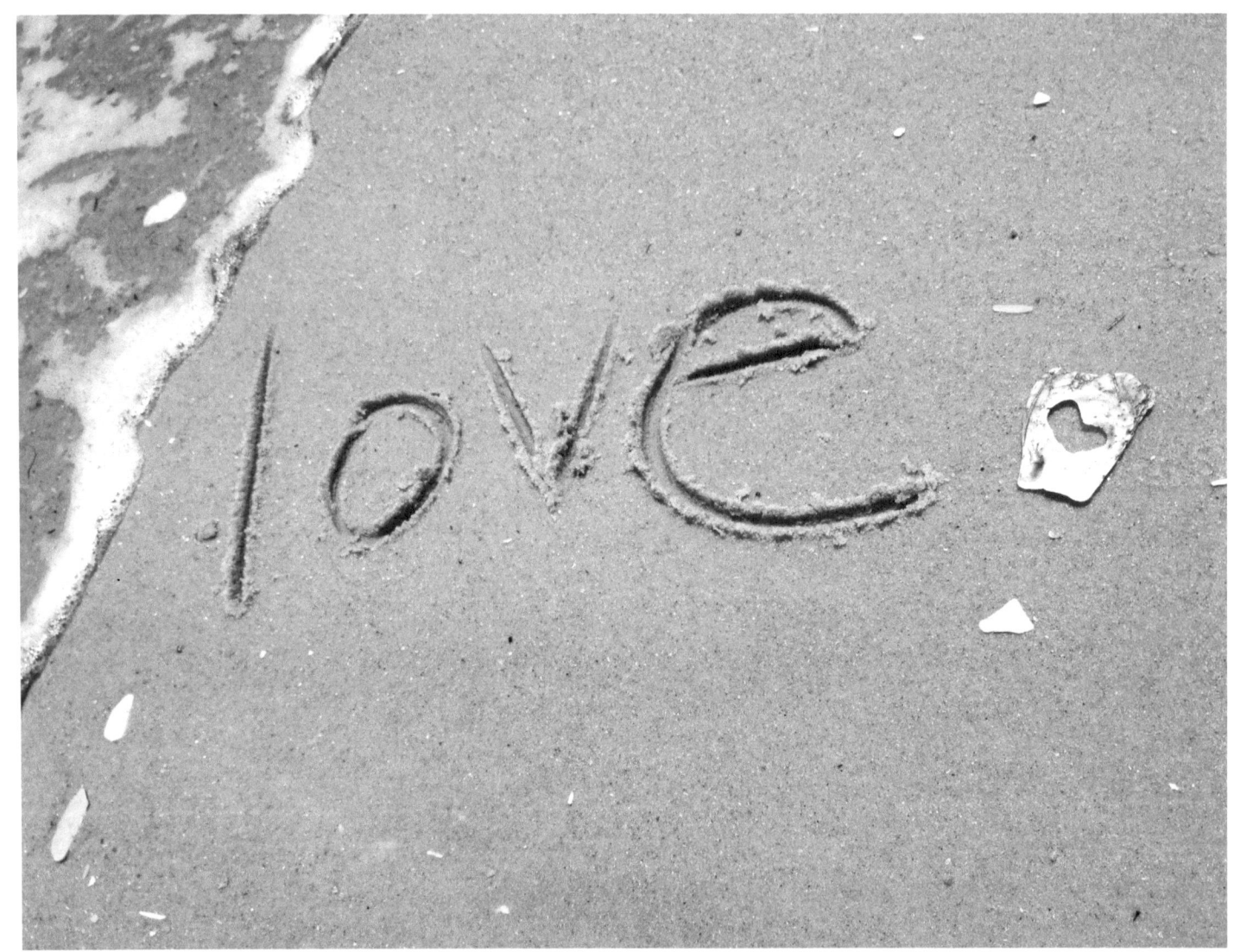

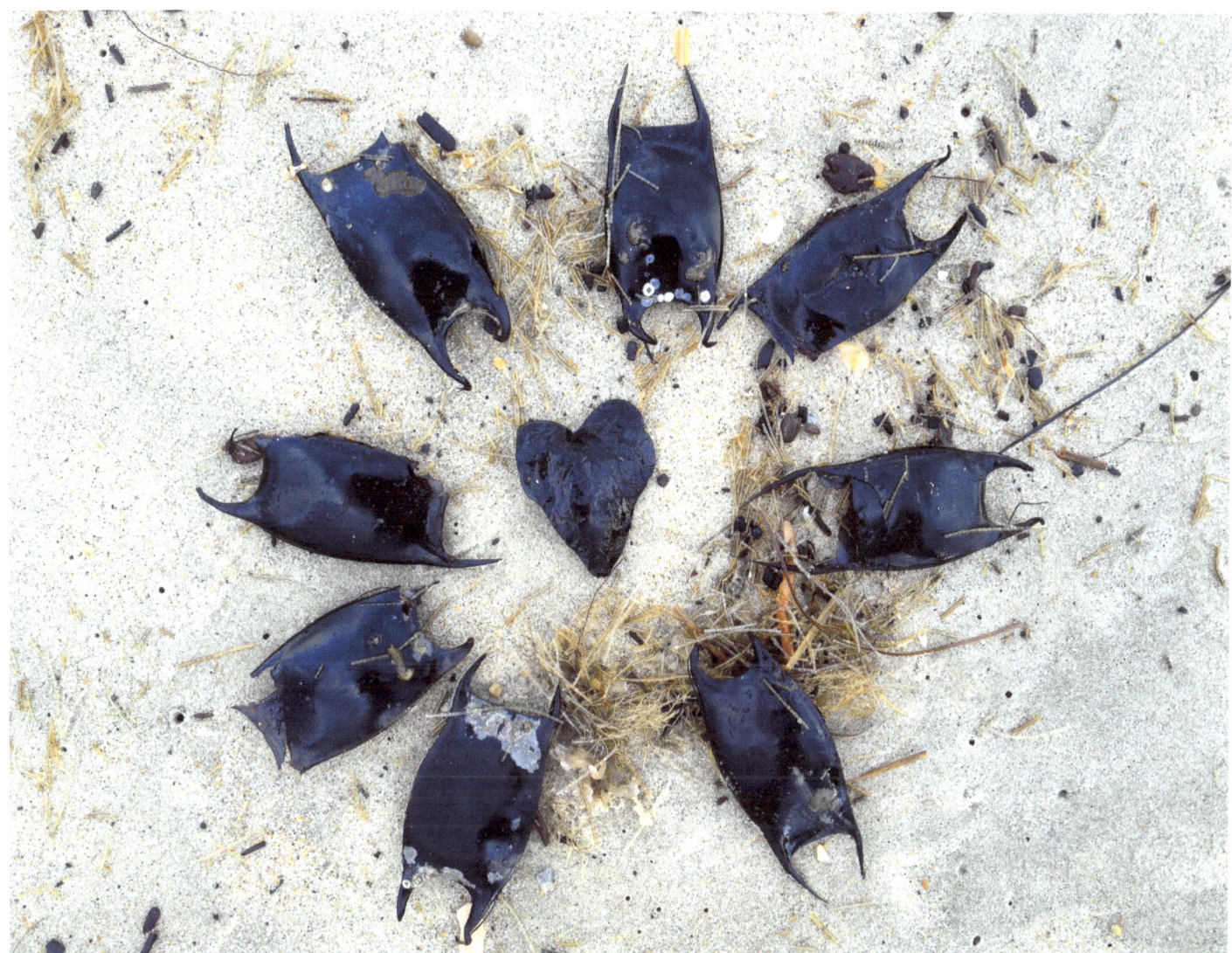

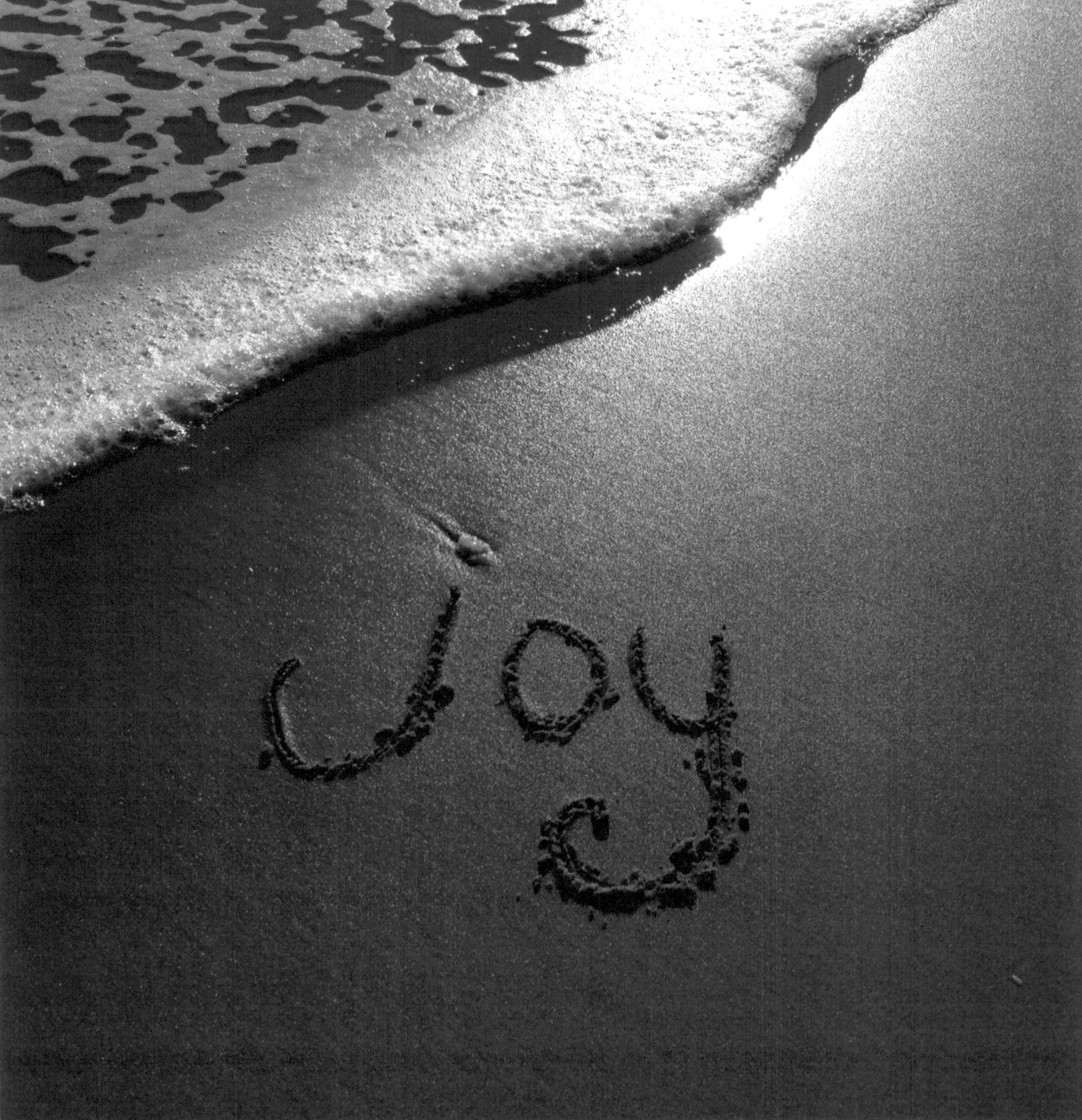

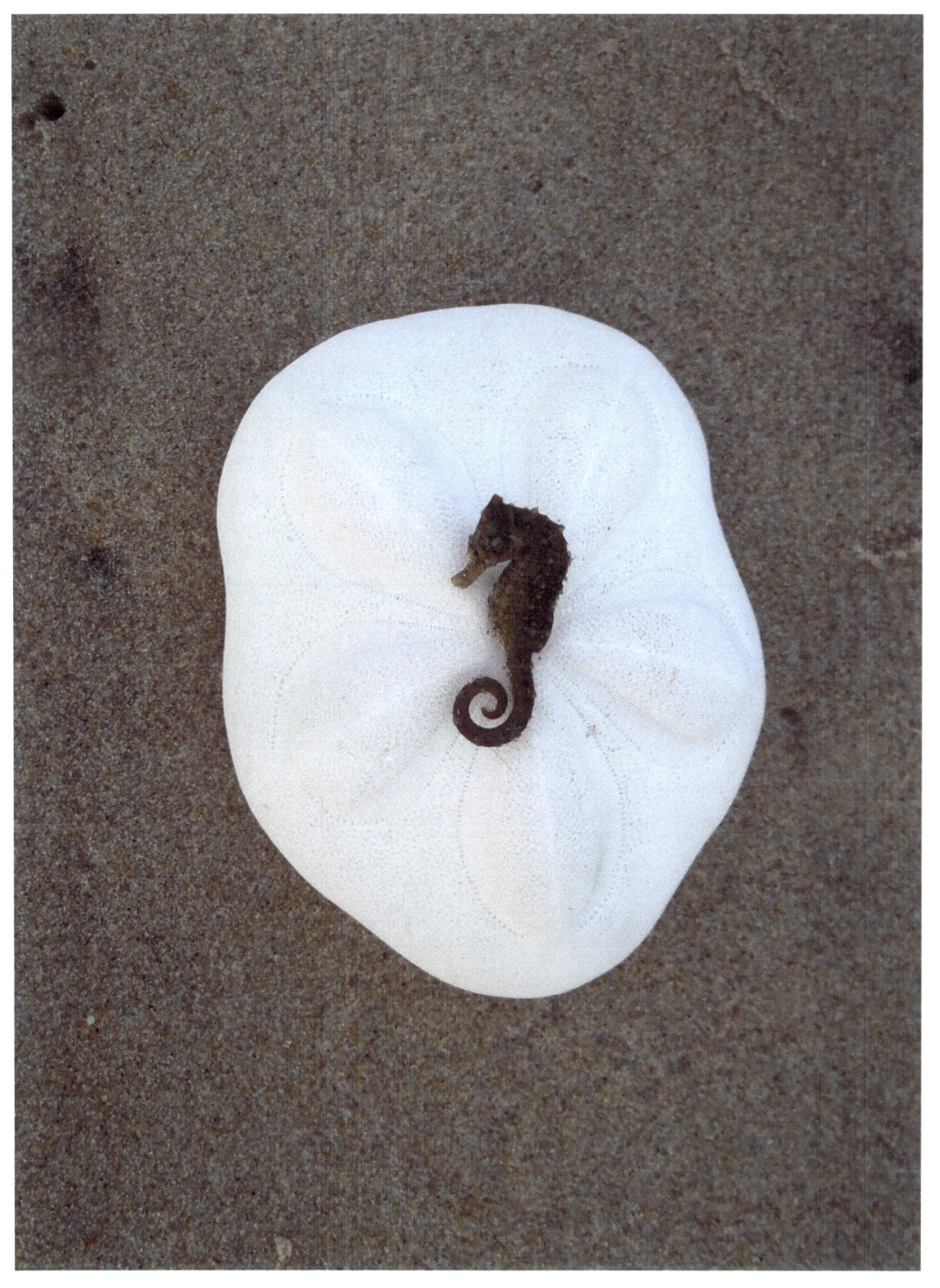

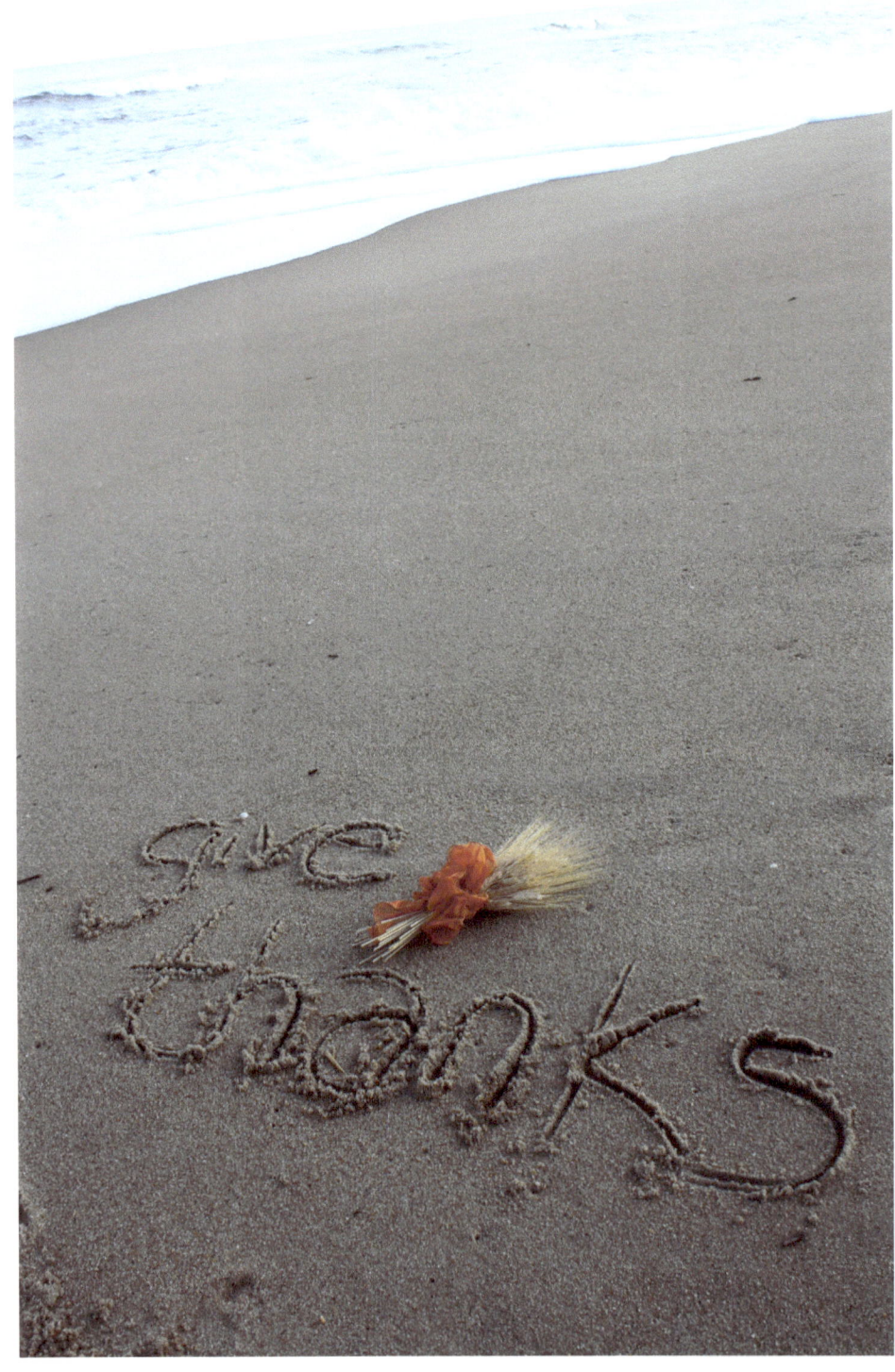

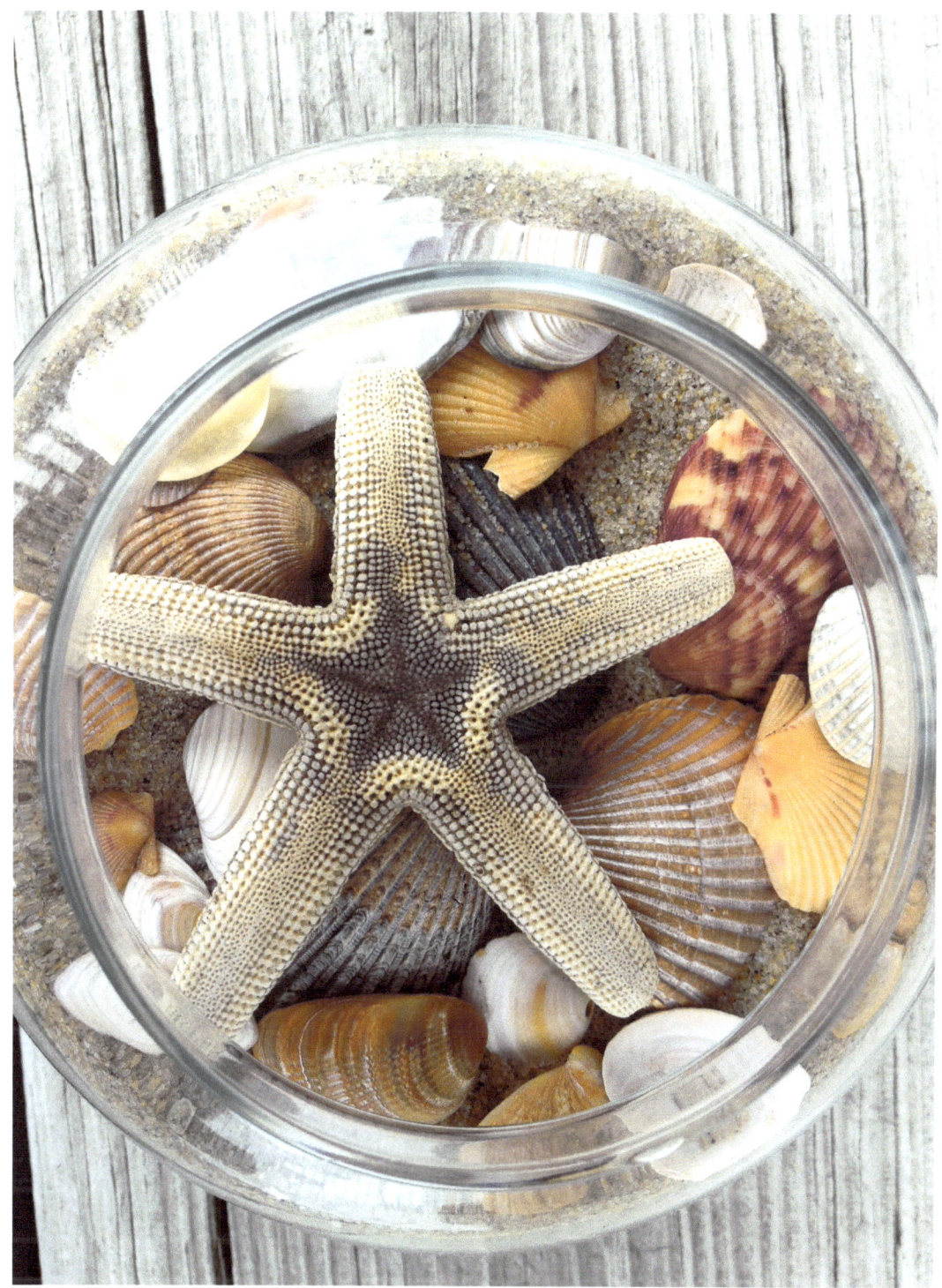

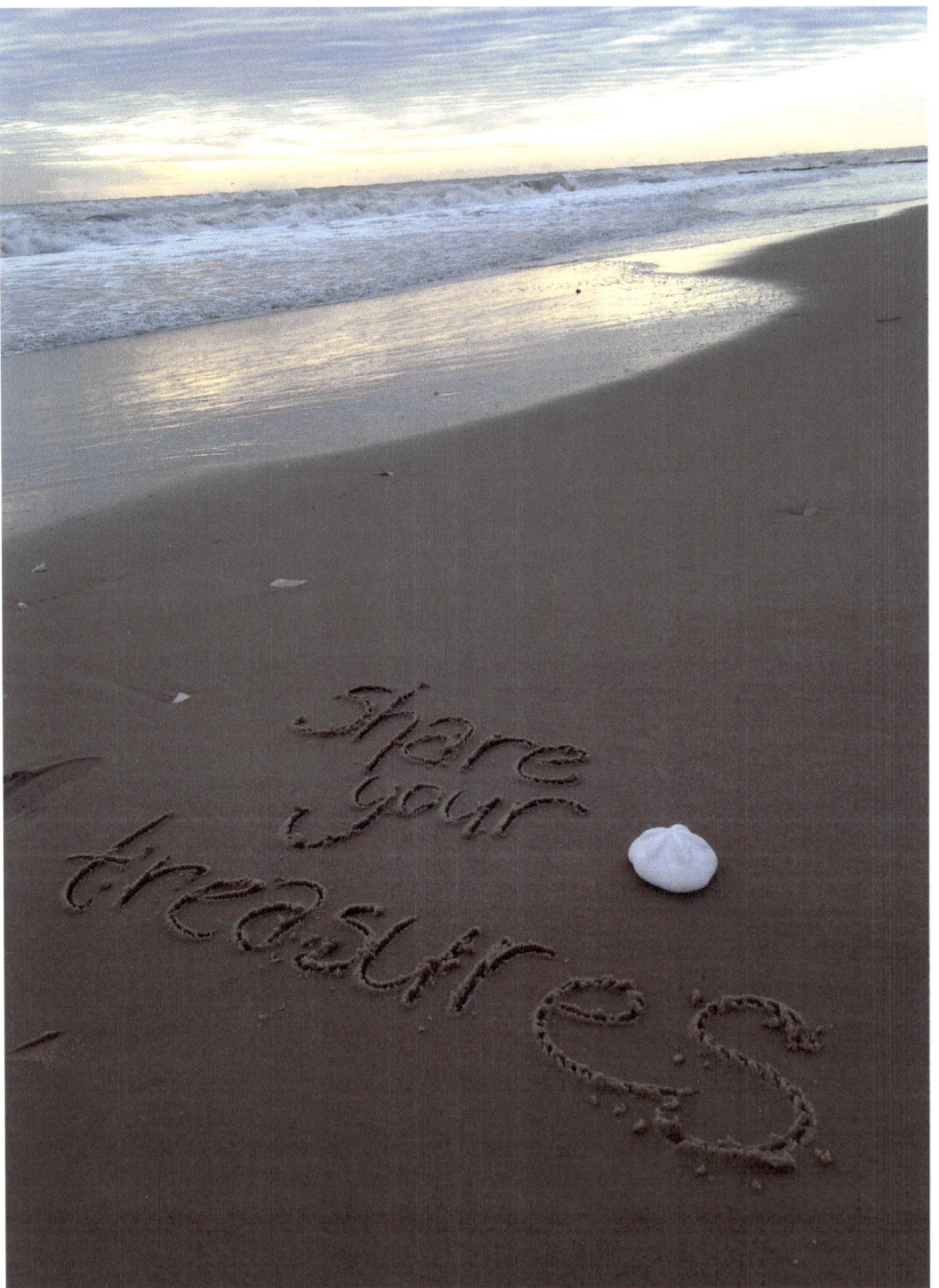

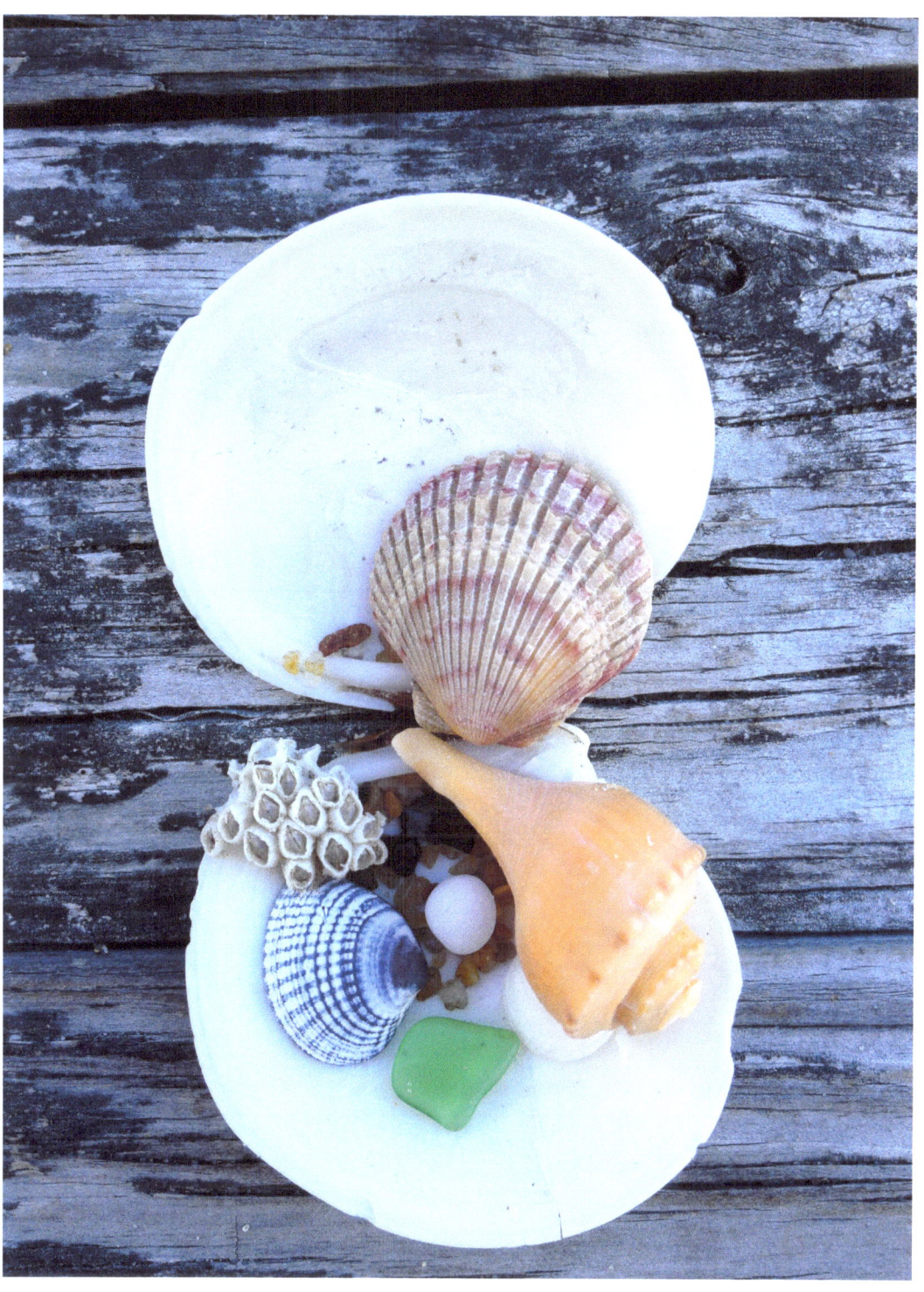

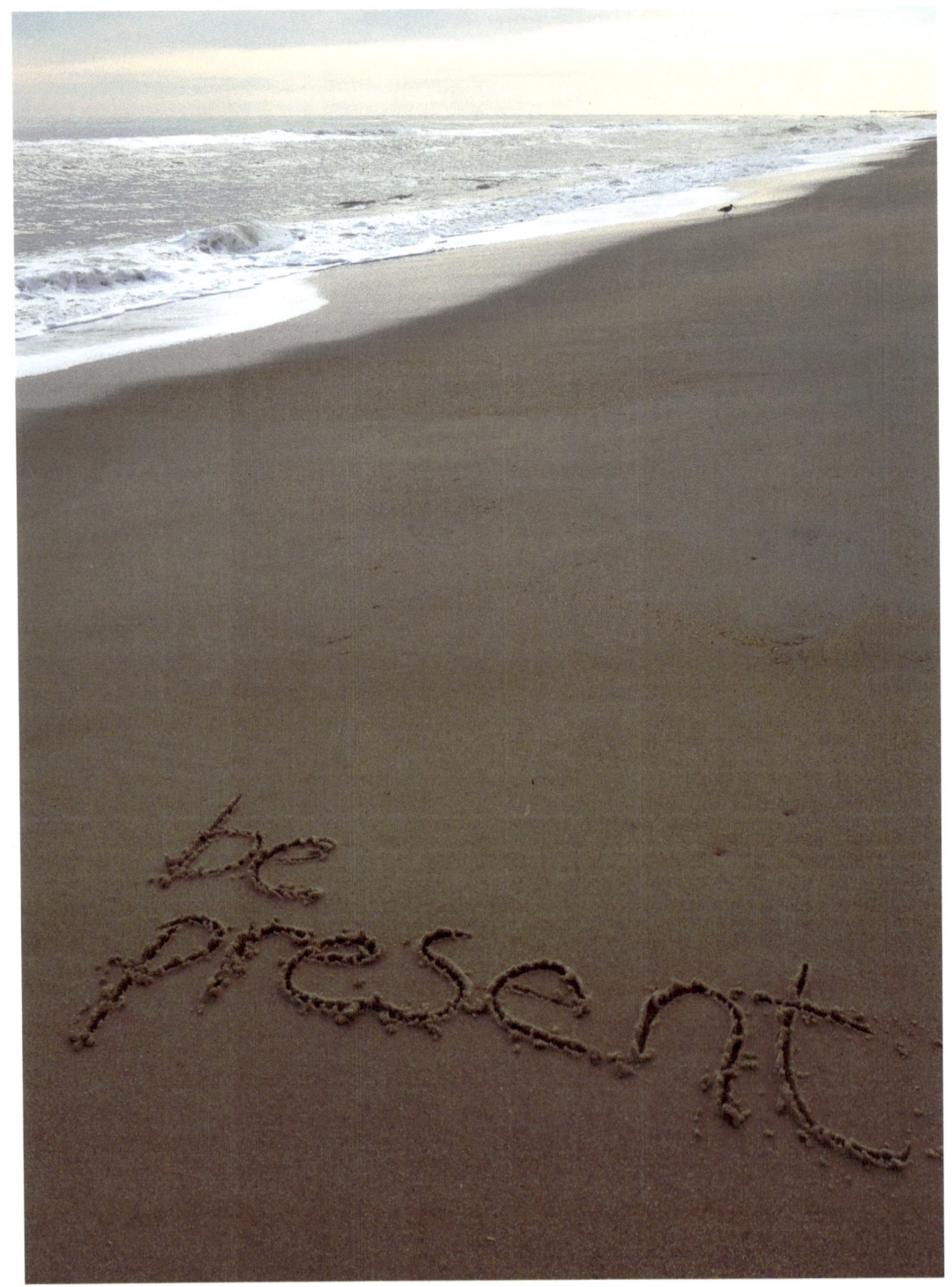

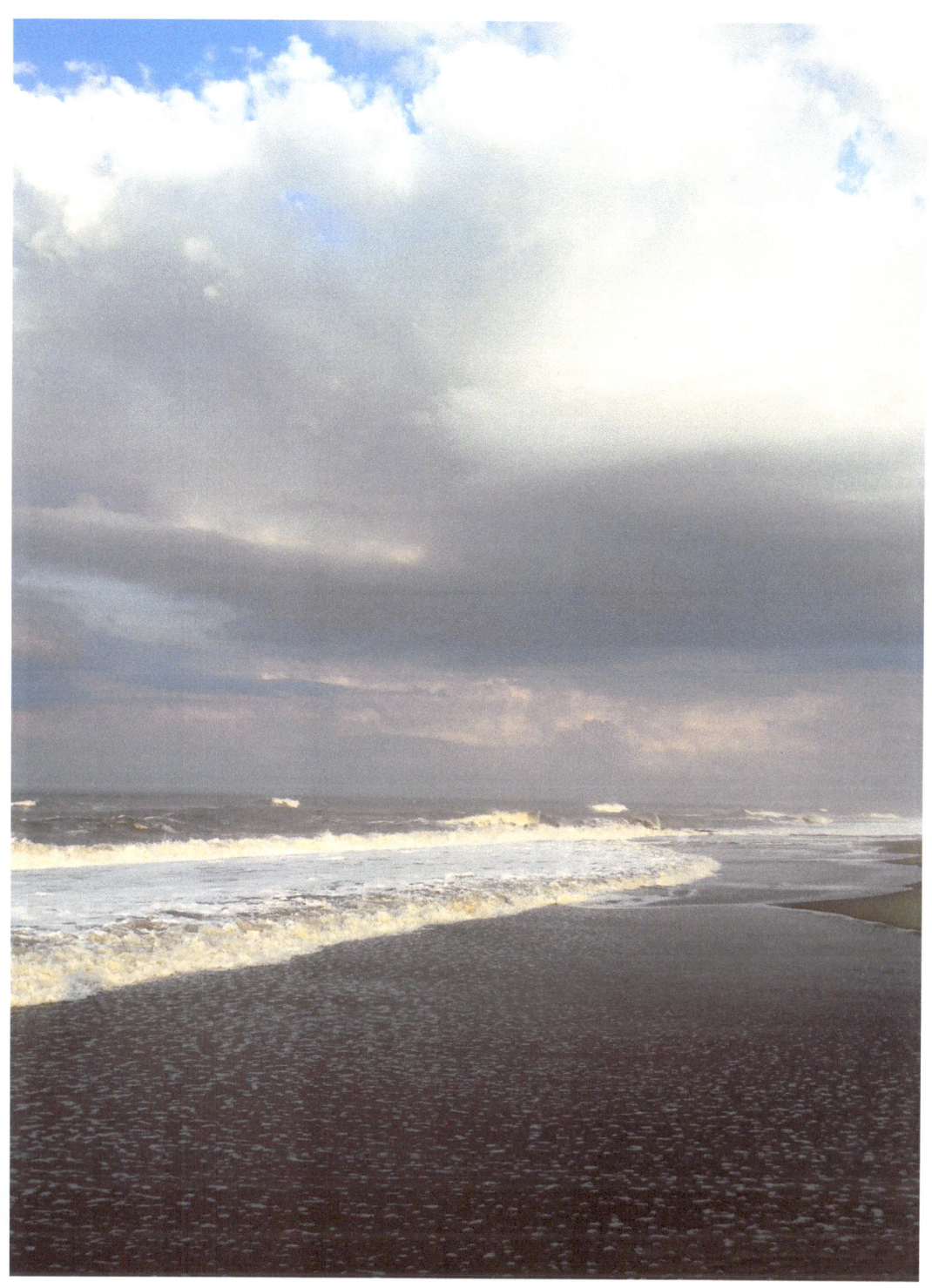

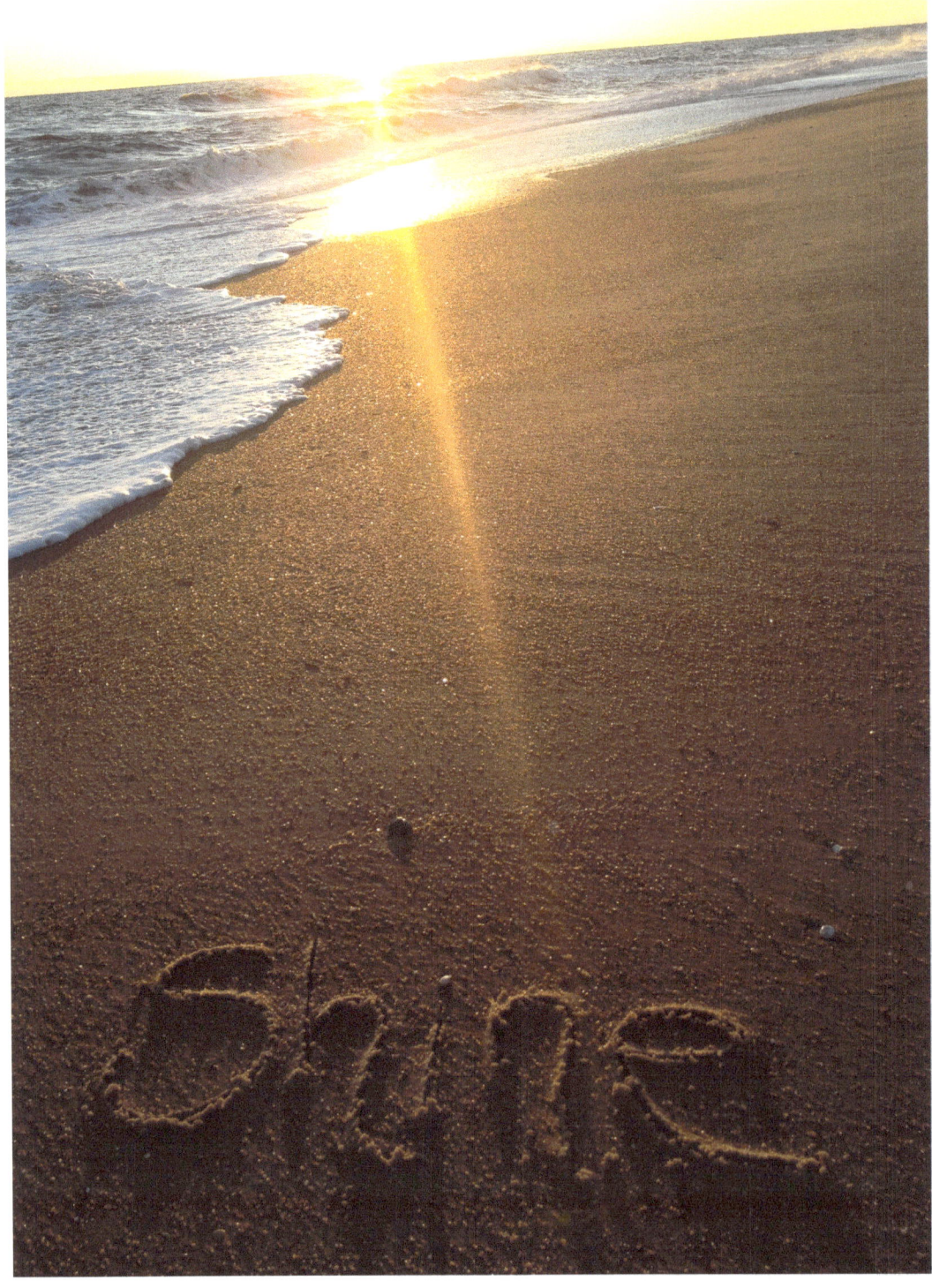

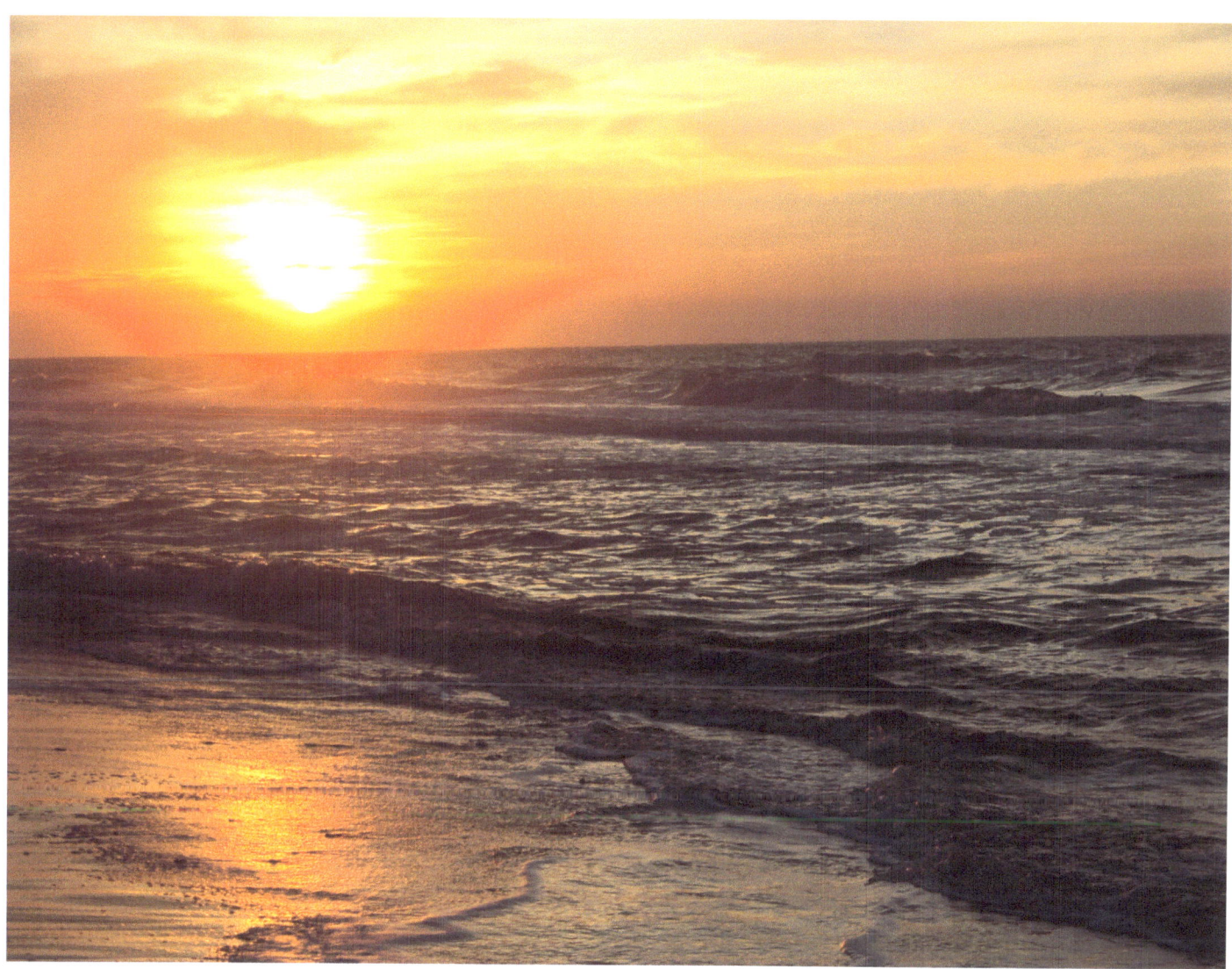

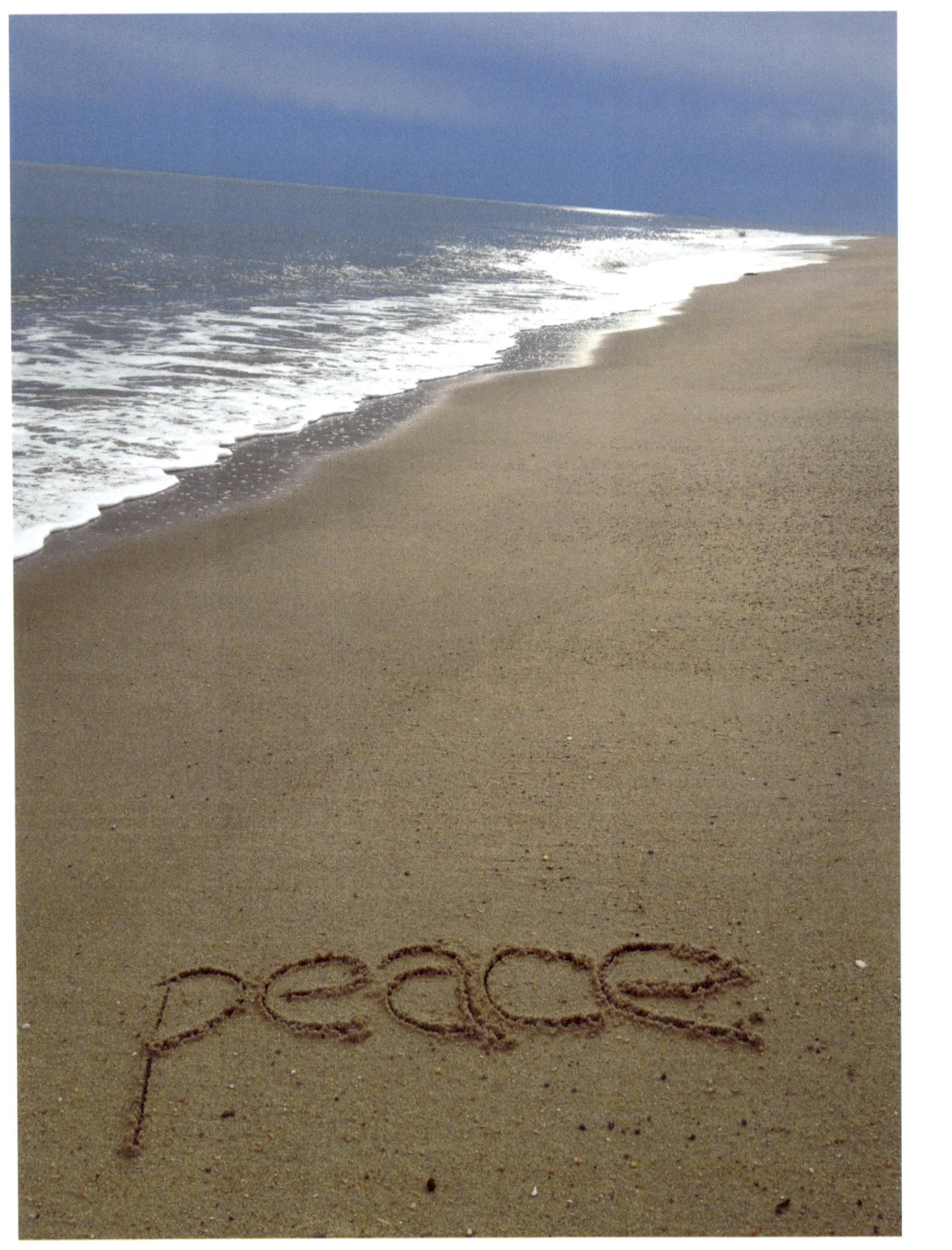

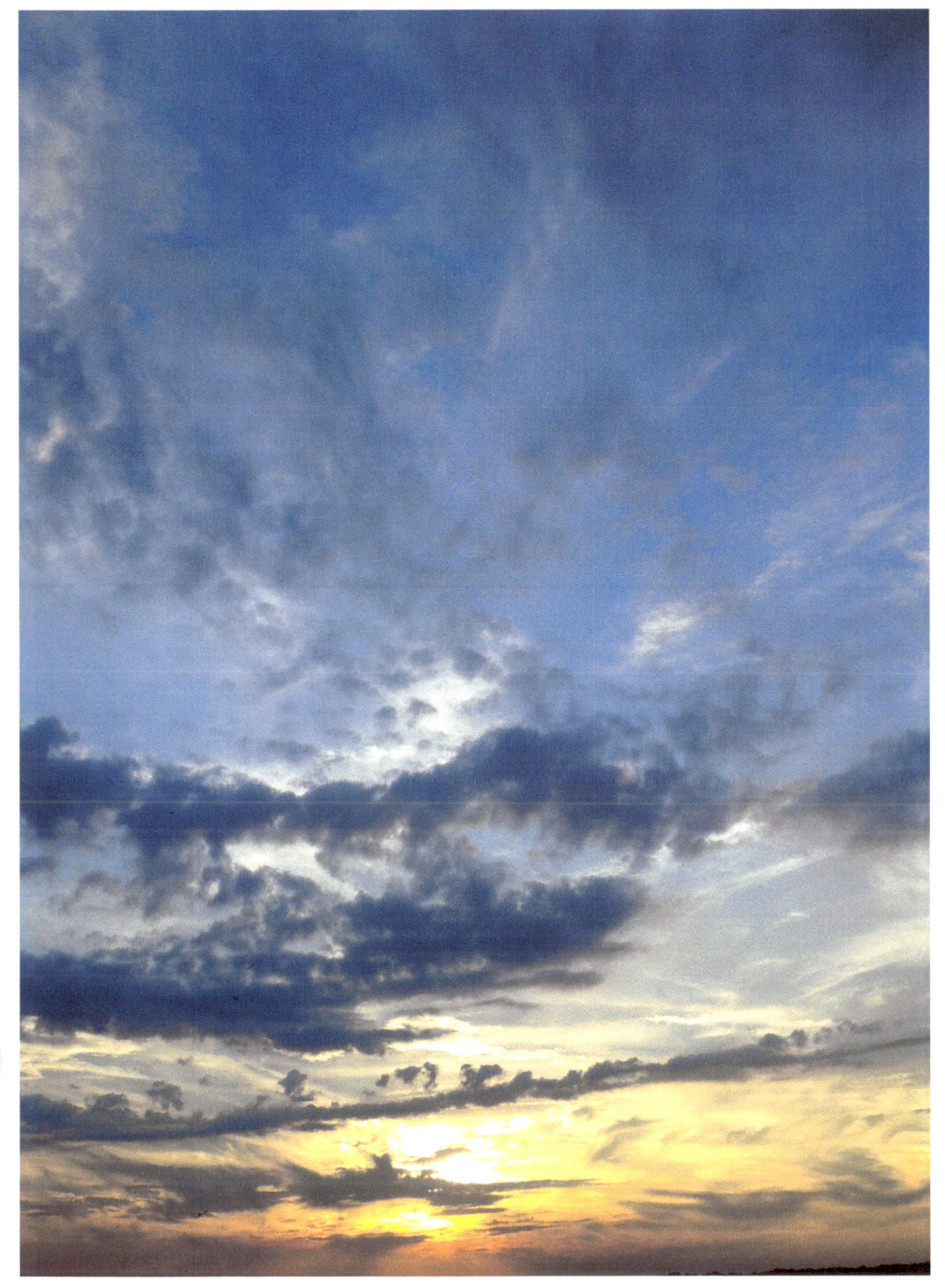

How my Beach Blessings journey began...

The beach is a place I return to again and again and the place I call home in my heart. It is the sacred and spiritual place where I feel most alive and most connected to myself and something greater. The ocean has always been

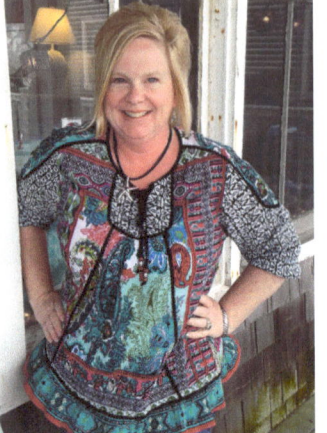

a source of peace, healing and inspiration for me. My wish is to share these blessings with you and pay tribute to the ocean and her offerings.

This book began over a year ago as I found myself writing the word "awaken" in the sand to welcome my "Artful Awakenings Retreat" guests. I have always loved the ocean and enjoy writing messages in the sand. This message created a wave of messages that I compiled along with other beach photographs to create the book you are holding in your hands.

Each time I visited the beach, I wrote several new messages in the sand and photographed them before they washed away. I tried to catch the light at sunrise or sunset, but also appreciated the dark, dramatic overcast days. I often got soaking wet as I waited for just the right moment to capture the shot. Sometimes my dog left little footprints across my words. Other times I would catch a stranger smiling at the message I had left behind. Sometimes I had the message already in mind as I headed to the beach. Other times, I let the ocean speak to me and scribed what I heard. Most of these "beach blessings" are messages, mantras, or affirmations that I incorporate into my artwork, share in my classes combining art and self-discovery or follow in my daily practice of personal and spiritual growth. I feel the ocean is a part of me and I have been listening to the voice of the ocean all my life. This project is my way of speaking back and giving thanks.

May you walk in peace wherever your journey leads and may your life be filled with love and light.

Blessings,

Jackie

I invite you to join my conversation with the ocean by writing and posting your own "beach blessings" to Instagram at *#beachblessings.*

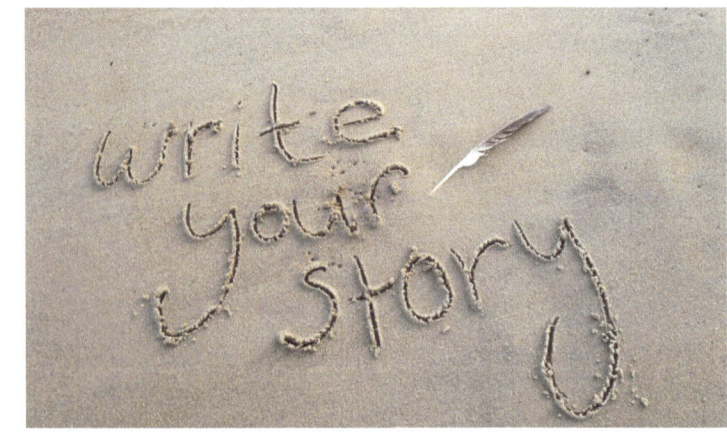

Jackie Tury is an artist, teacher, retreat leader and beach lover. To see more of Jackie's work go to: *www.jackietury.blogspot.com*

www.ingramcontent.com/pod-product-compliance
Lightning Source LLC
Chambersburg PA
CBHW050836180526
45159CB00004B/1920